Joan of Arc

JOAN OF ARC
by
JULES MICHELET

Translated,
With an Introduction,
by
Albert Guérard

Ann Arbor Paperbacks
THE UNIVERSITY OF MICHIGAN PRESS

First edition as an Ann Arbor Paperback 1967
Copyright © by The University of Michigan 1957
All rights reserved
ISBN 0-472-06122-4
Published in the United States of America by
The University Michigan Press
Manufactured in the United States of America

1992   *9 8*

Introduction

"He was not mistaken when he claimed he had done for Joan of Arc that which could never be done again. His book remains the only one by a gifted writer, the only one that possesses life, which combines rationalism and tradition; more accurately, rationalism and fideism (which is faith in the potency of faith). Such a combination is arbitrary, and it is unstable in the highest degree; but in the course of his work, Michelet displays such tenderness, he gives evidence of such a moving sympathy for suffering, of such a righteous faith in noble causes, that scholarly criticism, after the most searching discussion, must acknowledge its limitations and yield to emotion for a while." [1]

These lines sum up Michelet as the historian of Joan of Arc. They were wrenched, as it were, from a man whose spirit and method were at the very antip-

[1] Gustave Rudler, *Michelet historien de Jeanne d'Arc* (Paris, 1926), II, 75.

v

odes from Michelet's. Rudler had written a remark-
able guide for research scholars, *The Techniques of
Literary History and Criticism in the Study of Modern
French Literature.*[2] He had given an excellent demon-
stration of his own precepts in his critical edition of
Michelet's *Jeanne d'Arc.*[3] Thus he was led to examine,
with the utmost rigor, the sources of information of
the great romantic historian, and the way in which he
had made use of them. His verdict was that, as a work
of erudition, Michelet's book was full of flaws, and
that, in the course of a century, it had been altogether
superseded; but also that it remains alive and unique.
The unique always has a touch of the arbitrary and the
precarious: only the commonplace is absolutely safe
and sane.

This unique virtue is not purely of a literary nature. Michelet has a great style of his own, faulty by
academic standards of taste and even of syntax; nerv-
ous, breathless at times, but direct, thoroughly honest,
spurning brilliancy, eloquence, affected profundity.
His *Joan of Arc*, with obvious blemishes, is a rare work
of art. But it is also an even rarer work of history, if
history be the resurrection of the past.

Joan of Arc stands, as Rudler pointed out, as a
miraculous blend; and it is my contention that only
through such a blend could the atmosphere of the time
and the soul of the Maid be recreated for us. The
scholars—Jules Quicherat, the greatest among them,

[2] Oxford, 1923.
[3] Paris, 1925. 2 vols.

Siméon Luce, Pierre Champion—leave us at the same time bewildered and cold. No living presence arises out of their masses of documents. The literary artists fail to convince us. Schiller is of course very noble, Anatole France properly ironical; Shaw displays his luminous common sense in paradoxical guise; Péguy reveals his tormented fuliginous soul, his strange, heavily shod, slogging mysticism, the unearthly lyrical notes that redeem his incredible and wearisome verbosity. They are great authors, but they are authors. They are using Joan as their subject. Michelet and Joan of Arc are one.

Jules Michelet was born in Paris, on August 21, 1798. He was of humble origin: his father, a printer in a small way, was ruined by Bonaparte's ruthless suppression of most newspapers. No wonder Michelet was never dazzled by the military show of the Empire, as were Béranger and Thiers or, on a higher level, Balzac and Victor Hugo. It was a heavy sacrifice for a working family to give their son the most thorough education. Conscious of their effort, the boy bore hardships with stoic pride, and took the habit of unremitting labor. He was a most conscientious craftsman: Rudler's severe scrutiny does not invalidate that fact. No doubt his great *History of France* was too vast an enterprise; yet it was not dashed off with the brilliant facility of an Alexandre Dumas. Michelet united a romantic love for the savor of original documents with

an infinite capacity for taking pains. As the Director
of the Historical Section in the National Archives, he
had access to the treasures of the past. In spite of all
the gaps, inaccuracies, and misinterpretation properly
listed by Rudler, Michelet was a pioneer in medieval
studies. Rough his knowledge might be, but it was es-
sentially sound. To the present day, the many correc-
tions in details do not affect the substantial truth of his
history.

Michelet's hard work was well rewarded. He took
his doctor's degree in 1819. From a mere tutor in a
modest private institution, he rose to be a teacher of
history at the Collège Sainte-Barbe. In 1827, he was
called to a professorship at the Ecole Normale Su-
périeure, which was then, and remains, France's finest
graduate school. He was a memorable teacher, at the
same time enthusiastic and scrupulous. In 1831, he was
given his position at the Archives. He was in every
sense a professional, recognized as such by his peers.

His vocation had come at a most opportune moment. For many reasons history was in high favor under the Constitutional Monarchy (1814–48): partly as
an escape from the timeless rationalism of the Enlight-
enment (yet it was Voltaire who had created *the New
History*), partly as a form of political reaction (the
Bourbons represented the force of tradition, the wisdom of prejudice), and partly as a romantic fondness
for the picturesque past (Chateaubriand had opened
the way, and the enormous vogue of Sir Walter Scott
was both a sign and a cause of that yearning for van-

ished glamour). The sovereigns of the age, whether they stood for legitimacy like Louis XVIII and Charles X, or for canny compromise like Louis Philippe, were equally drab. Under these stodgy old men, France—and the whole of Europe—dreamed of knights in resplendent armor.

Michelet, whose religious and political convictions were still in a fluid state, found himself at home in the conservative atmosphere of the Restoration. He may not have been an ardent royalist, but he was not a declared republican. He was a sincere Catholic: all the more so because he had come to the Church late and with his eyes open; he was not baptized until he was eighteen. In his formative years he grew profoundly attached to the past, and that attitude of mind survived the liberal revolution of 1830.

He did not go straight to the task of his whole life, his mighty *History of France*. He sought his way and enriched his mind with a number of miscellaneous works, an *Epitome of Modern History* (1827–29), a translation of Vico's *Scienza nuova* under the title *Introduction to Universal History* (1831), a *History of the Roman Republic* (1831). Not one of these is indifferent; but their chief value was as a preparation for his *magnum opus*. Intensely patriotic, he never was parochial. If his *Joan of Arc* is written with the directness, the simplicity of a chronicle, the presence of a philosophical mind is felt in every page. His appointments at Normale and at the Archives focused his mind and gave him his opportunity.

The medieval part of his *History* was published from 1833 to 1844, in six volumes. The fifth, which appeared in 1841 and was devoted to the reign of Charles VII, contained the three chapters on Joan of Arc. They stood out from the very first as Michelet's masterpiece. He published them separately in 1853; the slim volume has remained a classic in France, and almost a gospel, for a whole century. Charles Péguy, most ardent among the worshipers of the Maid, never allowed a doubt as to the primacy of Michelet.[4]

Exactly at that time, Michelet and many of his

---

[4] French literature had been singularly unfortunate in its treatment of the Maid. Villon had struck the right note, but in two lines only:

> And Joan the good Lorrainer
> Whom the English burned at Rouen. . . .

Ronsard, in the hope of writing a national epic, a French *Aeneid*, picked out as his hero Francus, son of Hector, instead of Joan of Arc. In the seventeenth century, Jean Chapelain (1595–1674), the official prince of French poets and critics, promised a *Pucelle* for which the world waited in confident admiration for twenty years. When the first twelve cantos appeared in 1656, they were hailed for a few months as "beautiful . . . if tedious." But soon the leaden epic plummeted into oblivion. The last twelve cantos were published, as an erudite curiosity, only in 1882. In the eighteenth century Voltaire had the atrocious bad taste to compose a scurrilous mock-heroic poem by the same title as Chapelain's, *La Pucelle*. Dull as its would-be sprightliness may seem to modern readers, it enjoyed for at least two generations a kind of scandalous subterranean fame. It must be said that in his *Philosophical Dictionary* and in his great universal history, *Essay on the Manners of Nations*, Voltaire speaks of Joan in decent and intelligent terms.

fellow romanticists—Lamartine, Hugo, George Sand
—lived in a sort of spiritual twilight. By this I do not
mean a crepuscular semidarkness, but the paradoxical
blending of two conflicting faiths. They were still
attached to the religion of their youth, and they would
have spurned the *make-believe* which is the stigma of
decadent romanticism; but their belief, for all its ear-
nestness, was dissolving into a will to believe. Soon it
would fade into a sympathy with faith, and then into
nostalgia for faith.

Not that they sank into indifference; but their
Christianity, under the influence of Lamennais, was
assuming a democratic, a humanitarian, a Promethean
tinge. The service of God, to them, was the service of
Man. For mankind, which God created in His own
image, and into which He breathed His very spirit,
was the collective incarnation of the divine. Christ was
God and the Son of God, *because* He was Man and the
Son of Man. Of this religious, democratic, and social
gospel, which throughout Europe led to the millennial
hopes of 1848, France was the appointed bearer;
France was a Christ among the nations.

Now the fifteenth century was likewise an age of
religious twilight: Villon's "Ballad to the Virgin" is a
window richly dight, illumined by the afterglow of
a setting faith. Joan of Arc was a daughter of the people; in the miseries of war, she thought first of the people, their infinite distress, "the great pity that was in
the kingdom of France." Her mission took a religious
form because she had been brought up in the ancient

faith. She was to save the people in the name of God, through God's chosen instrument, His vicar on earth, the Lord's Anointed, the king of France, who *was* France. Thus democracy, social pity, the tradition of the French crown from the anointing of Clovis to Charlemagne and St. Louis, were fused into a single glowing religion which the quibbles of theologians could never compass. On the earthly plane she had her hour of triumph, her Palm Sunday, but she failed and suffered death. Out of her martyrdom, not out of her victories, came France's redemption. With no thought of turning his *Joan of Arc* into a Faulknerian *Fable,* Michelet had the gospel story constantly in mind.[5]

About 1840, Michelet was still enough of a Catholic for such a faith not to be repellent to him. He had moved away from orthodoxy, but he could still hear the bells, "like a mother's gentle reproof." There is an admirable paragraph[6] in which he bids a tender, a dolorous farewell to the Church of his young manhood. This paragraph he deleted in the edition of 1853, yet it gives the key to the whole work. The Michelet of 1853, committed to anticlerical free thought and radical republicanism, could not have identified himself with Joan of Arc. He would either have spurned her "superstition," or overpraised her rebellion against the hierarchy, the Church militant. In 1840 he was in

[5] The martyred Messiah was one of the great Romantic themes, either in the Promethean form, or in the Christian. Even Napoleon was transfigured into that pattern: St. Helena became either a Caucasus or a Golgotha.

[6] "The Temptation," pp. 94–95.

full sympathy with the creative, the thaumaturgic power of her faith; and he also felt to the full the ambiguities which must have preyed obscurely on the soul of Joan herself.

Already he had turned his chair at the *Collège de France* (1838) into a pulpit, where he preached his new democratic humanism. He was about to publish a series of books (*The Jesuits*, 1843; *The Priest, Woman and The Family*, 1845; *The People*, 1846) which, powerful as they may be, were works of religious and political controversy, not of serene science. He had transferred his allegiance from medieval theocracy (God as the king of France, the earthly king as His vicar) to democratic theocracy: *vox populi*. The French Revolution became in his mind a myriad-headed Messiah. The white heat of his passion and his masterly—not to say masterful—handling of original documents made his *History of the French Revolution* (eight vols., 1847–53) another triumph of resurrection through the magic of sympathy. He alone, not Taine, Madelin, or Gaxotte, not even Aulard or Mathiez, makes us understand the *spirit* of the Revolution. Indifference benumbs, hatred kills, love alone creates life.

Then came the great hope and the great frustration of 1848. Under the Second Empire, he was among the defeated. Deprived of his official positions, he lived in uncompromising opposition and moral exile. His *History of France from the Sixteenth Century to the Revolution* (ten vols., 1855–67) was the prolonged and tragic cry of a great wounded soul. He found comfort in a happy second marriage, and in delightful books of poetic natural history, *The Bird*, *The Insect*, *The Sea*, *The Mountain*.

The war of 1870 was to him a staggering blow. Not merely because his beloved France was humbled and scourged, but because the second home of his spirit, the Germany of the philosophers, musicians, and poets, was defiled. Kant, Beethoven, and Schiller faded, and he had to face the Gorgon head of Bismarckian brutality: *might is right*. When Paris capitulated, he suffered an apoplectic stroke.

He conquered his ailing body, resumed work, wrote the first three volumes of his *History of France in the Nineteenth Century* (1872). He died at Hyères on February 9, 1874.

He had labored with incredible industry and devouring ardor for well over fifty years. The English-speaking world knows him but dimly: Edmund Wilson's tribute, in *To the Finland Station*, gave a shock of surprise. The inevitable clumsiness of translations —the present one not excepted—obscures the strange and elusive beauty of his style. For the orthodox he is merely a French infidel; for the dryasdust, a hopeless romanticist; the realist, Marxist as well as Manchesterian, would brand him as starry-eyed. But he is the purest, the most ardent apostle of that Promethean faith, humanistic and universal, generous and free, the faith of Schiller and Shelley, so often defeated so constantly derided, which still embodies man's best hope.

Contents

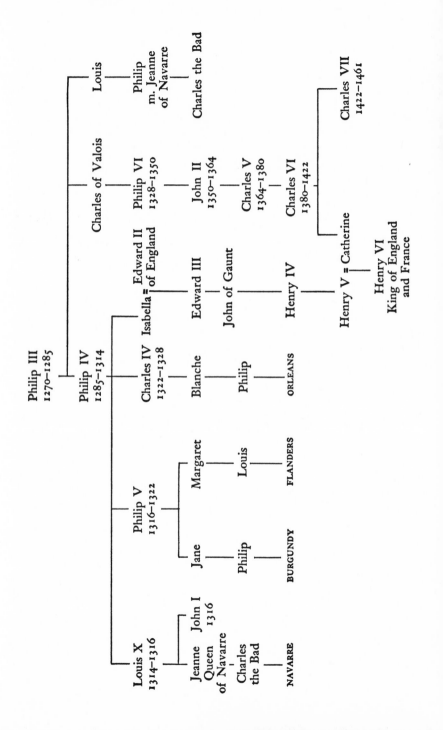

Philip III
1270–1285

Philip IV
1285–1314

Louis X
1314–1316

Philip V
1316–1322

Charles IV
1322–1328

Isabella = Edward II
of England

Charles of Valois

Louis

Jeanne   John I
Queen   1316
of Navarre

Charles
the Bad

NAVARRE

Jane   Margaret

Philip   Louis

BURGUNDY   FLANDERS

Blanche

Philip

ORLEANS

Edward III

John of Gaunt

Henry IV

Henry V = Catherine

Henry VI
King of England
and France

Philip VI
1328–1350

John II
1350–1364

Charles V
1364–1380

Charles VI
1380–1422

Charles VII
1422–1461

Philip
m. Jeanne
of Navarre

Charles the Bad

Joan of Arc

I

Childhood and Vocation of Joan

Joan's eminent originality was her common sense. This sets her apart from the multitude of enthusiasts who, in ages of ignorance, have swayed the masses. In most cases, they derived their power from some dark contagious force of unreason. Her influence, on the contrary, was due to the clear light she was able to throw upon an obscure situation, through the unique virtue of her good sense and of her loving heart. The shrewd and the cautious, the men of little faith, could not unravel the knot: she cut it. She declared in the name of God that Charles VII was the rightful heir. He himself doubted his legitimacy; she reassured him. She secured for that legitimacy the sanction of Heaven by leading her king straight to Reims; and through her swift action she won over the English the decisive advantage of the coronation.

It was not rare for women to take up arms. They frequently fought in beleaguered cities—witness the

thirty women wounded at Amiens, witness Jeanne
Hachette.[1] In the lifetime of the Maid, in those very
same years, the women of Bohemia were fighting by
the side of their men in the Hussite wars.

Neither is the uniqueness of the Maid to be
sought in her visions. Who did not have visions in the
Middle Ages? Even in this earthy fifteenth century,
excessive sufferings had led to a strange exaltation.
We find in Paris a Friar Richard stirring the populace
with his sermons, to such a point that the English had
to drive him out of the city. Masses of fifteen or
twenty thousand men, at Courtrai, at Arras, thronged
to hear the Breton Carmelite Conecta. Within a few
years, before and after the mission of the Maid, mystics
appeared in every province, claiming inspiration.
Among them were Pierrette, a Breton girl who held
converse with Jesus Christ, Marie of Avignon, and
Catherine of La Rochelle. Saintrailles brought from
his countryside a shepherd boy who bore the stigmata
on his feet and his hands, and who sweated blood in
Holy Week, as happens in our own day with the
Blessed Woman of Tyrol.

Lorraine was, it would seem, one of the last
provinces where such a phenomenon was likely to oc-
cur. The Lorrainers are brave, they are born fighters,
but they are inclined to be wily and crafty. If the great
duke of Guise [2] saved France before he became a cause

[1] The heroine of the siege of Beauvais, 1472, Jeanne Laisné,
called "the Hatchet."

[2] François of Lorraine, duke of Guise, *le Balafré* ("Scar-
face"), recovered Calais and started the religious wars, 1519–63.

of dissension, he was not moved by visions. We find two Lorrainers at the siege of Orleans; both display the puckish humor of their spirited compatriot Callot. One was Master John, the gunner who could sham death so expertly. The other was a knight who, captured and shackled by the English, returned to his own side when they left, riding on the back of an English monk.

The part of Lorraine abutting on the Vosges Mountains, on the other hand, is of a sterner kind. These French highlands, whence rivers flow in every direction to every sea, were covered with forests so vast that the Carolingians thought them best fitted for their imperial hunts. In the clearings of these forests rose the venerable abbeys of Luxeuil and Remiremont; the latter, as the reader knows, was governed by an abbess who was a princess of the Holy Roman Empire. She had her great dignitaries, a full-fledged feudal court, and her seneschal marched ahead of her, bearing a naked sword. For a long period, the duke of Lorraine was the vassal of this female overlord.

It was precisely between the Vosges region of Lorraine and the region of the plains, between Lorraine and Champagne at Domremy, that the fair and valiant maiden was born who was destined to carry so gloriously the sword of France.

There are four Domremys within ten leagues along the river Meuse; three in the diocese of Toul, one in the diocese of Langres. It is probable that in earlier times these four villages had been domains of the Abbey of St. Remy at Reims. Our great abbeys, it is well known, held possessions still farther afield, even in Provence, even in Germany, even in England. The line of the Meuse, the borderland between Lorraine and Champagne, was bitterly contested between the king and the duke. Joan's father, Jacques Darc, was a worthy Champenois. It seems that Joan inherited her disposition from him; we find in her no trace of Lorraine asperity, but rather the gentleness of Champagne, a blend of simplicity, good sense, and shrewdness such as we encounter in Joinville.

A few centuries earlier Joan would have been born a serf of the Abbey of St. Remy; a century before, a serf of the Sire of Joinville, for he was the lord of the town of Vaucouleurs, of which the village of Domremy was a dependency. But in 1335 the king had compelled the Joinville family to cede Vaucouleurs to him. It was at that time on the main route from Champagne to Lorraine, the direct highway into Germany; and not only on the road to Germany, but on the road along the Meuse, and so at the crossing of the ways. It was also, so to speak, the boundary of the contending factions; there was, not far from Domremy, one last village belonging to the Burgundian party; all the rest acknowledged Charles VII. This "march" or borderland between Lorraine and Champagne had constantly and cruelly suffered from the wars: long warfare between East and West, between the king and the duke, for the possession of Neufchâteau and the surrounding strongholds; warfare between North and South, between

Burgundians and Armagnacs. The memories of these implacable wars could never be effaced. Not very long ago they were still pointing out near Neufchâteau a tree centuries old, and with a sinister name, a tree whose branches must have been laden with many a human fruit, *the oak of the partisans.*

The unfortunate inhabitants of the borderlands had the honor of being the direct subjects of the king; that meant in fact that they belonged to no one, were supported by no one, were spared by no one: their only liege, their only protector, was God. People under such circumstances grow sober-minded; they know that their hold on goods or life is precarious. They till the soil, the soldiery take the harvest. Nowhere is the peasant more deeply concerned with the affairs of the whole country; his immediate interests are at stake; the least repercussions of national conflicts are felt with shattering force. So the peasant seeks information; he tries to know, to anticipate; but he is resigned to whatever may come, he expects the worst, he is patient and of a stout heart. Even the women grow brave; and they have to be, among all those soldiers, if they are to defend their life and their honor, like Goethe's fair and robust heroine, Dorothea.

Joan was the third daughter of a peasant, Jacques Darc or d'Arc, and of Isabelle Romée.[3] She had two godmothers, one called Joan, and the other Sybil.

The eldest son had been baptized Jacques, an-

---

[3] In the Middle Ages, those who had gone on a pilgrimage to Rome often assumed the name *Romée.*

other, Peter. The pious parents named one of their daughters after a more exalted saint, John.[4]

While the other children went with their father working in the fields or watching the flocks, her mother had Joan stay with her, and kept her busy sewing and spinning. She learned neither to read nor write; but she was taught everything that her mother knew about the things that are holy. Her religion came to her, not as a lesson or a ceremony, but in the folklike and naïve form of a lovely tale told of an evening, like the simple faith of a mother. That which we thus receive with our blood and our milk is a living thing, is life itself.

We have a touching testimony about Joan's piety, that of her childhood friend, her bosom friend, Haumette, younger than she by three or four years. "How often," Haumette says, "I went to her father's house and slept with her in loving friendship. . . . She was a very good girl, simple and sweet. She loved to go to church, and to holy places. She would spin and do household chores like other girls. . . . She went to confession frequently. She blushed when she was told that she was too devout, that she went to church too often." A peasant, who was also called as a witness,[5] adds that she nursed the sick and gave alms to the poor. "I know it for certain," he said; "I was a child then, and she took care of me."

[4] In a somewhat fanciful note, Michelet implies that the name John had mystic connotations.
[5] In Joan's second trial, for the revision of the first.

Every one was aware of her charity, her piety. All could see that she was the best young girl in the village. One thing they did not know: that in her the life of the spirit dominated, absorbed the lower life, and held in check its vulgar infirmities. Body and soul, she was granted the heavenly grace of remaining a child. She grew up to be robust and handsome; but the physical curse of women never affected her. This was spared her, to the benefit of religious thought and inspiration. Born in the shadow of the church, lulled by the canticle of the bells, fed on legends, she was a legend herself, swift and pure, from her birth to her death.

She was a living legend. . . . But the vital force in her, exalted and concentrated, became all the more creative. Unawares, the young girl *created*, so to speak, her own ideas, turned them into realities, made them entities, powers, imparted to them, from the treasure of her virginal life, an existence so splendid, so compelling that the paltry realities of this world grew faint in comparison.

If *poetry* means *creation*, this no doubt is supreme poetry. We must enquire by what degree she reached such a summit, and from what a humble beginning.

Humble indeed, but poetical from the first. Her village was but a stone's throw from the great forests of the Vosges. From the door of her father's house she could see the old grove of "The Oaks." That wood was the haunt of fairies; they loved above all a fountain near a huge beech tree which was called "the tree of the Fairies," or "of the *Ladies*." Little children came there to hang wreaths and to sing. Those ancient "Ladies," once mistresses of the forest, were no longer permitted, it was said, to foregather by the fountain; they had been banished thence because of their sins. The Church, however, was constantly on her guard against the old divinities of the place; the priest, to keep them away, came once a year to say mass at the fountain.

Joan was <u>born in</u> that <u>atmosphere of legend</u>, of folklike dreamings. But the countryside offered another and very different kind of poetry, fierce, atrocious, and, alas! all too real: the poetry of war . . . <u>War</u>! That single word sums up all the emotions; not every day was marked by assault and pillage; but rather by the anguished expectancy, the tolling of the alarm bell, the sudden awakening, and, far in the plain, the sullen glare of fire. . . . A horrible condition: yet with an aura of poetry; even the most down-to-earth of men, the Lowland Scots, turned into poets amid the perils of the *Border;* from that blasted heath, which still seems under a curse, the ballads blossomed forth like wild and vigorous flowers.

Joan had her shares in those romantic experiences. She saw the poor refugees drift in; she, in her kindness, helped receive them; she yielded her bed to them and slept in the hayloft. Her parents too were once compelled to flee. Then, when the flood of brigands had swept past, the family returned, found the village ransacked, the house plundered, the church gutted by fire.

Thus she realized the full meaning of war. She understood this anti-Christian condition; she was horror-stricken at this Devil's misrule under which every man dies in a state of mortal sin. She asked herself whether God would permit this to go on forever, whether He would not put an end to all this misery, whether He would not send a liberator, as He had so often done to save Israel, a Gideon, a Judith? . . . She knew that more than once a woman had saved God's chosen people; that it was said in the beginning that woman would crush the serpent's head. She could see in the portals of churches St. Margaret with St. Michael trampling the dragon underfoot. . . . If, as everyone was saying, the kingdom had been ruined through a woman (Isabelle of Bavaria), an unnatural mother, then salvation might come through a virgin. And this is exactly what Merlin had prophesied; this prophecy, enriched, transformed in the various provinces, had taken a purely Lorraine cast in Joan's own country. It was a maiden from the marches of *Lorraine* who was destined to redeem the kingdom. The prophecy had received this added touch as a result of the recent marriage of René of Anjou with the heiress of the duchy of Lorraine, a union which in fact was very favorable to France.

One summer day, a day of fasting, at noon, as Joan was in her father's garden close to the church, she saw in that direction a dazzling light and heard a voice, "Joan, be a good and dutiful child; go often to church." The poor girl was greatly alarmed.

Another time, she heard the voices once more, saw the radiance, but within the light there were noble figures; one of them had wings, and seemed to be a knight wise and loyal (*prud'homme*). He said to her, "Joan, go thou to the assistance of the king of France, and thou shalt restore his kingdom to him." She answered, trembling, "Sir, I am but a poor village maiden; I could not ride a horse, or lead men-at-arms." The voice replied, "Thou shalt go to M. de Baudricourt, Captain of Vaucouleurs, and he shall have thee conducted to the king. St. Catherine and St. Margaret will come to thy aid." She stood amazed and in tears, as though she had envisioned her whole destiny.

The *prud'homme* was none other than St. Michael, the stern archangel of judgments and battles. He returned, restored her courage, told her of "the great pity in the kingdom of France." Then came the white figures of the saints, amid lights innumerable, their heads adorned with rich coronets, their voices so sweet and tender that tears welled in her eyes. But Joan wept most of all when the saints and the angels left her. "Dearly I wished," she said, "that the angels had taken me with them."

If she wept, in such great happiness, it was not without cause. Fair and glorious as these visions were, they transformed her life. Hitherto she had heard but one voice, that of her mother, of which her own voice was but the echo; now she heard the mighty voice of the angels! . . . And what was the will of that voice from heaven? That she should leave her mother, the home so dear to her. She who was so easily abashed even by a single word, she would have to go among men, speak to men, to soldiers. She would have to face the hostile world, and war, and leave her little garden in the shadow of the church, where no sound reached her except the voice of the bells, where birds came to feed out of her hand. For such was the magic of the young saint's gentleness that animals and the birds of heaven came to her, as they did to the anchorites of old, trusting in the peace of God.

Joan told us nothing about this first conflict. But it must have taken place, and it lasted for a long period, for five years elapsed between her first visions and the time she left her father's house.

The two authorities, that of her father, that of heaven, gave conflicting commands. The one wanted her to remain in obscurity at her humble work; the other ordered her to go and save the kingdom. The angel told her to take up arms; her father, a blunt downright peasant, swore that rather than see his daughter run away with the men-at-arms, he would drown her with his own hands. One way or the other she would have to disobey. This without doubt was her hardest battle; in comparison, her encounters with the English would be only child's play.

Her family, in its opposition, tried to tempt her away from her call. They assayed to get her married, in the hope that she would in this wise be reconciled with saner ideas. A young man in the village claimed that, when she was a child, she had promised to marry him; and as she denied it, he had her summoned before the ecclesiastical judge of Toul. They hoped she would not dare to defend herself, that she would rather allow herself to be condemned, and to be married. To everyone's great astonishment, she went to Toul, appeared before the court, spoke in her own defense, she who hitherto had been so silent.

In order to escape from the authority of her family, she had to find within that very circle someone who had faith in her; that was the hardest task. As she could not reconcile her father to her mission, she managed to win over her uncle. He took her away with him, on the pretext that his wife, who was lying in, would need her. She prevailed upon him to go to Squire de Baudricourt, Captain of Vaucouleurs, and solicit his support. The rough soldier gave the peasant a surly welcome; there was nothing to be done, he said, except to take her back to her father's house, after slapping her face soundly. She was not discouraged; she had made up her mind; and her uncle was obliged to go with her. This was the moment of decision; she was leaving her village and her family forever; she kissed her girl friends good-bye, and especially her little darling Mengette, whom she commended to the grace of the Lord; but as for her bosom friend and companion, Haumette, whom she loved best of all, she had not the heart to see her again.

So she came to the town of Vaucouleurs, in her peasant dress of coarse red stuff; she and her uncle took lodgings with a wheelwright, whose wife grew very fond of Joan. She had herself conducted to Baudricourt, and told him with firmness "that she had come with a commission from her Lord that he should send word to the dauphin to hold fast, and not to engage in any battle with his enemies, because the Lord would send him succor by Mid-Lent. . . . The kingdom did not belong to the dauphin, but to her Lord; and it was the Lord's will that the dauphin should become king, and hold the kingdom in trust." She added that in spite of his enemies, the dauphin would be made king, and that she would have him anointed.

The captain was greatly surprised; he suspected the devil had a hand in all this. He consulted the parish priest who, it seems, shared his misgivings. She had not mentioned her visions to any cleric. The priest, then, came with the captain to the wheelwright's house; he unfolded his stole, and admonished Joan to depart, if she were the envoy of the Evil One.

But there was no room for doubt in the minds of the common folk; they were filled with wonder. From all sides they flocked to see her. A gentleman said, in order to probe her, "Well, sweet friend! It looks as though the king were to be chased away, and we must be turned into Englishmen." She complained to him about Baudricourt's refusal. "And yet," she said, "before Mid-Lent I must be with the king, even though to get there I had to wear my legs down to my knees. For no one in the world, no kings, no dukes, no daughter of the king of Scotland, can reconquer the kingdom of France. I alone can bring succor, though I should prefer to stay at home by my mother's side, and spin; for this is not my work; but go I must, and accomplish it, for such is the will of my Lord."— "And who is your Lord?"—"It is God." The gentleman was moved. He pledged her his faith, his hand in her hand, that "under God's guidance he would take her to the king." A young gentleman also felt his heart touched, and declared that he would follow this holy Maid.

It would seem that Baudricourt sent to the king for his consent. Meanwhile, he led her to the duke of Lorraine, who was sick and desired to consult her. All he got from her was the advice to appease God by seeking reconciliation with his wife. In spite of this reproof, he encouraged her.

When she returned to Vaucouleurs, she found there a messenger from the king, granting her permission to come. Another battle had been lost, and the dauphin's advisers were in a mood to try every possible means. Joan had told of the fight the very day it was waged. The people of Vaucouleurs, not doubting her mission, collected money to provide her with equipment and a horse. The captain gave her nothing but a sword.

There was one last obstacle to conquer. When her parents were told of her approaching departure, they nearly went out of their minds; they made desperate efforts to hold her back; they used commands and threats. She withstood this last ordeal, and had someone write a letter to them, begging their forgiveness.

It was a hard and perilous journey that she was now setting out upon. The whole countryside was harried by troops of both parties. There were no roads and no bridges left; the rivers were in flood; it was February in the year 1429.

Thus to venture forth with five or six men-at-arms was enough to fill a girl with fear and trembling. An English or a German woman would never have risked it: the *indelicacy* of such a step would have filled her with horror. Joan felt no misgivings: she was too pure to entertain any fear of that kind. She had assumed the garb of a man, and was to wear it to the last; such clothes, tight-fitting, strongly fastened, would be her best protection. Yet she was young, and fair to look upon. But she was hedged round, for those who saw her at closest quarters, with a barrier of religious awe; the youngest of the gentlemen who escorted her declared that, sleeping near her, he never felt even the shadow of an impure thought.

With heroic serenity, she traversed this stricken land, either deserted or infested with soldiers. Her companions regretted at times that they had set out with her; some thought that perhaps she was a witch after all; they were sorely tempted to desert her. But her mind was so thoroughly at peace that, in every town, she wanted to stop and hear mass. "Have no fear," she would say, "God is preparing my path; it is for this I was born." And again: "My brothers in paradise tell me what I have to do."

The court of Charles VII was far from unanimous about the Maid. This inspired girl, coming from Lorraine, encouraged by the duke of Lorraine, would inevitably strengthen the party of the queen and her mother, the party of Lorraine and Anjou. An ambush was set against the Maid some distance from Chinon, and it was a miracle that she escaped.

So strong was the opposition that, when she arrived, the council debated for two days whether the king should see her. Her enemies hoped to adjourn the affair indefinitely by deciding that information should first be sought in her own country. Fortunately, she had friends also, the two queens undoubtedly, and above all the duke of Alençon. Until recently he had been in the hands of the English, and he was anxious to carry the war northward, so as to recover his duchy. The people of Orleans, to whom ever since the twelfth of February Dunois [6] had been promising this assistance from heaven, sent messages to the king, urging that the Maid should come.

At last the king received her, surrounded with richest pomp; some had evidently hoped that she would be disconcerted by all this array. It was evening; fifty torches lighted the hall; many nobles, more

[6] Jean, Count of Dunois, was in command of the French forces at Orleans.

than three hundred knights, were gathered round the king. Everyone was anxious to see the witch, or the inspired Maid.

The witch was eighteen; she was a handsome girl, and attractive, fairly tall, with a gentle voice that went to the heart.

She presented herself humbly, "like a poor little shepherdess"; she picked out the king at the first glance, although he had on purpose mingled with the crowd of the nobles; and although he denied at first that he was the king, she clasped his knees. But, as he had not yet been anointed, she called him only dauphin. "Gentle dauphin," she said, "my name is Joan the Maid. The King of Heaven brings you word through me that you shall be anointed and crowned in the city of Reims, and that you shall be the lieutenant of the Heavenly King, Who is the king of France." The king took her aside, and after a moment's conversation, a change came upon their countenances; she was telling him, as she related later to her confessor, "My Lord has sent me to tell thee that thou art indeed the *true heir* of the French kingdom, and *the son of the king*."

Another thing that caused amazement, with a tinge of fear, was that the first prediction she made, as if casually, was fulfilled at the very moment. A man-at-arms, struck with her beauty, voiced his evil lust, with a round sacrilegious oath, after the manner of soldiers. "Alas!" she said, "that you should forswear your God, when your death is so near!" A short while afterward, he fell into the water and was drowned.

Her enemies objected that her foreknowledge might be inspired by the devil. Four or five bishops were brought together to examine her. They were probably reluctant to commit themselves, so divided was the court between the factions; so they advised that the inquiry be made at the University of Poitiers. There were in that great city a university, a *Parlement* or high court of justice, and a crowd of learned men.

The archbishop of Reims, chancellor of France, chairman of the king's Council, summoned doctors and professors of theology, some of them secular priests, the others members of religious orders, and commissioned them to examine the Maid.

After the doctors had been brought into the hall and duly seated, the girl sat down at the end of a bench and answered their questions. With lofty simplicity, she told them of the apparitions and the words of the angels. A Dominican offered a single objection, but a weighty one, "Joan, you say it is the will of God to deliver the people of France; if such be His will, He has no need of soldiers." She was not disturbed: "Well," she said, "the soldiers will do the fighting, and God will give them victory."

Another examiner proved harder to satisfy, a certain Brother Séguin, professor of theology at the University of Poitiers, "a very sour man," the chronicle reports. He asked her, with his thick Limoges brogue, what language it was that the alleged celestial voices used? Joan answered, with a touch of impatience, "Better than yours, at any rate." "Do you believe in God?" said the incensed doctor. "Well, it is not God's will that we should accept your word, unless you show us a sign." She answered, "I have not come to Poitiers to give signs or perform miracles; my sign will be to raise the siege of Orleans. Give me the men-at-arms, and I shall go."

Meanwhile, at Poitiers as at Vaucouleurs, her saintliness was manifest to the common people; in a moment, everyone was on her side. The women, gentle and simple, went to see her at the house where she was staying with the wife of an advocate before the *Parlement,* and they returned deeply moved. Even men went; councilors, lawyers, tough old judges were dragged thither, reluctant and skeptical, and when they had heard her, they wept even as the women did, and said, "This Maid is sent of God."

The examiners themselves went to see her, with the king's equerry; and they started over again their unending probe, plying her with learned quotations, demonstrating to her that, according to all the sacred authorities, she was not to be believed. "Listen," she told them, "there is more in God's book than in all of yours . . . I do not know A or B; but I came by God's command to raise the siege of Orleans and have the dauphin anointed at Reims. . . . But first I must write to the English, and summon them to depart. God so wills it. Have you paper and ink? Write; I am going to dictate: 'You, Suffort, Classidas and La Poule (Suffolk, Glasdale and de la Pole), I order you, in the name of the Heavenly King, to return to England. . . .'" They wrote obediently: she had taken possession of her very judges.

They gave as their opinion that it was lawful to use her services; and the same answer came from the archbishop of Embrun, who had been consulted. The prelate cited the fact that repeatedly God had revealed to virgins, for instance to the Sibyls, that which He had kept hidden from men. It was not in the devil's power to make a pact with a virgin; it was necessary, therefore, to ascertain whether Joan was a virgin indeed. So science, driven into a corner, unable or unwilling to pass upon the delicate distinction between holy and satanic inspirations, referred a matter of the soul to a test of the flesh, made this grave spiritual problem depend on the mystery of a woman's body.

As the doctors were nonplussed, it was the matrons who decided. The good queen of Sicily, the king's mother-in-law, with a few other ladies, took charge of this ludicrous examination: it turned out to the honor of the Maid. Some Franciscans, who had been sent out to gather information in Joan's country, returned with the most favorable reports. There was not a moment to lose. Orleans was crying out for help; Dunois was sending entreaty after entreaty. The Maid was equipped; some sort of household or retinue was arranged for her. First they appointed as her equerry a worthy knight of mature years, Jean Daulon, the most discreet gentleman among the retainers of Count Dunois. She had also a page of noble birth, two heralds, a steward, two valets; her brother Peter came and joined her train. As her confessor, they chose Friar John Pasquerel, an Augustinian hermit.

It was with wonder that the spectators beheld for the first time Joan of Arc in her white armor and on her beautiful black charger, by her side a small battle-ax and the sword of St. Catherine. She had directed that sword to be sought behind the altar of St. Catherine of Fierbois; and there it was found, as she had told. She carried in her hand a white standard with the royal lilies of France; on that standard God was represented with the world in His hands; on either side, an angel holding a lily. "I will not," she said, "use my sword to kill anyone." And she added that, much as she loved her sword, her standard was "forty times" dearer to her.

Let us compare the two contending parties at the moment she was sent to Orleans.

The English were greatly weakened as a result of a long winter siege. After the death of Salisbury, many men-at-arms whom he had enlisted thought they were released and went away. On the other hand, the Burgundians had been recalled by their duke. When the French stormed the main English *bastille* or fortified position, into which the defenders of several other bastilles had retreated, only five hundred men were found. All in all, it seems that there were only two or three thousand men on the English side, and of that small number not all were Englishmen; there were also a few Frenchmen, whom the English probably did not trust overmuch.

If the English had been concentrated, they would have formed a force to be reckoned with; but they were scattered in a dozen bastilles or bulwarks; and between these, in most cases, there was no communication. This arrangement proves that Talbot and the other English leaders had hitherto been served by their courage and their luck rather than by their military skill. It was obvious that every one of these little fortified places, in its isolation, would be helpless against the large and stout city they were attempting to subdue; that this numerous population, grown warlike in the course of the long siege, would in the end besiege its besiegers.

When we scan the formidable list of the captains who had thrown themselves into Orleans, La Hire, Saintrailles, Gaucourt, Culan, Coaraze, Armagnac; when we note that in addition to the Bretons of Marshal de Retz and the Gascons of Marshal de St. Sévère, the captain of Châteaudun, Florent d'Illiers, had roused the nobility of the region to join him in this local expedition, the relief of Orleans seems less of a miracle.

It must be said, however, that one thing was lacking for these great forces to be effective, a thing that was essential, indispensable: unity of action. Dunois might have provided it, if skill and cleverness had sufficed. But they were not enough. What was needed was an authority: more than the king's authority, for the king's captains had lost the habit of obeying the king. To curb these wild and wilful men, God Himself must take command. The God of that age was the Virgin, far more than Jesus. The Virgin was needed, a Virgin descending upon earth in the guise of a maid from the common folk, young, fair, gentle, and bold.

Protracted warfare had changed men into wild beasts; now it was necessary to change these brutalized creatures into men again, into Christians, into obedient subjects. A great transformation, and difficult! Some of those Armagnac captains were perhaps the most ferocious men that ever lived. One name is enough, a horrendous name: that of Gilles de Retz, the prototype of Bluebeard.

Yet there was still one way of acting upon those dark souls; they had sunk below humanity, below nature, but they had not completely discarded religion. The brigands, it is true, managed to reconcile in the most bizarre fashion their religion and their brigandage. One of them, the Gascon La Hire, made this startling remark, "If God became man, He would be a pillager." And when he went after loot, he offered his little Gascon prayer, without saying too explicitly what he wanted, trusting that God would take the hint: "Sire God, I pray Thee to do for La Hire what La Hire would do for Thee, if Thou wert a captain, and La Hire were God."

It was a ludicrous and touching spectacle to see the sudden conversion of these old Armagnac brigands. They did not mend by halves. La Hire no longer dared to swear; the Maid took pity on his excessive strain, and allowed him to swear "by his baton," or staff of command. The devils, all of a sudden, had turned into little saints.

First of all, she demanded that they should send away their wild women, and that they should go to confession. Then, on the way, along the Loire, she had an altar erected in the open, she took communion, and they took communion. The loveliness of the season, the charm of springtime in Touraine, must have added greatly to the religious power of the young girl. The old soldiers felt young again; they blotted out the memories of their sinful years, they found themselves as they once were, in their happier times, full of good will and hope; all of them young as she was young, all like little children. . . . With her, they started a new life, with hearts full of joy. Whither was she leading them? They did not care. They would willingly have followed her, not merely as far as Orleans, but as far as Jerusalem. And the English were welcome to join them in the quest; in the letter she wrote to them, she offered them graciously to unite with the French, and, all together, to go and redeem the Holy Sepulchre.

II

Joan Delivers Orleans and Has the King Anointed at Reims

The first night they slept in camp she lay down in full armor, as she had no woman with her; but she was not yet accustomed to such hardships, and they made her ill. The thought of peril never entered her head. She wanted to cross over to the north bank of the Loire, the English side, and go through the system of English bastilles, affirming that the enemy would not budge. The leaders of the army paid no heed to her; they followed the other bank, so as to cross the river two leagues above Orleans. Dunois came out to meet them. "I am bringing you," she said, "the best assistance that ever came to any one, the help of the Heavenly King. Not I am bringing help, but the Lord Himself, Who, on the prayers of St. Louis and St. Charlemagne, took pity on the city of Orleans, and would not suffer that the enemies should possess both the body of the duke and his city."

She entered the town at eight in the evening, on

April 29; her progress was slow, for the great multitude made it difficult for her to advance. The people vied with one another in touching at least her horse. They looked at her "as though they were seeing God." While speaking to them with gentleness, she went as far as the church, thence to the home of the treasurer of the duke of Orleans, an honorable man whose wife and daughters made her welcome; she slept that night with Charlotte, one of the daughters.

She had entered the town with the supplies; but the army went down the river again, to cross it at Blois. Nevertheless, she was all for attacking the English bastilles at once. She had to be content with sending to the northern bastilles a second summons to surrender; then she had the same message delivered to the southern ones. Captain Glasdale heaped coarse abuse upon her, calling her "cowkeeper" and "common trull." In fact, they thought she was a witch, and were sorely afraid of her. They had not sent back her herald, and were considering whether they should burn him, in the hope of breaking the charm. However, they thought they had better first consult the doctors of the University of Paris. Dunois threatened to kill in retaliation the English heralds who were in his hands. As for the Maid, she felt no fear for her herald; she sent another one with the message, "Go and tell Talbot that if he takes up arms I shall do likewise. . . . Let him have me burnt, if he can catch me."

As the army was delaying, Dunois ventured to

sally forth in quest of it. The Maid, remaining in Orleans, found herself in sole control of the city: all other authorities seemed to have vanished. She went riding around the walls, and the folk followed her without fear. The next day, she went to inspect the English bastilles at close quarters; the whole populace, men, women and children, went with her to look at those dreaded forts, where nothing was astir. She brought the crowd back to Holy Cross, the cathedral, in time for vespers. She wept during church services, and everyone was likewise in tears. The people were beside themselves; they had cast off all fear; they were drunk with religion and war, in one of those formidable fits of fanaticism during which men are ready to do anything, to believe anything, hardly less terrible to their friends than to their foes.

The chancellor of Charles VII, the archbishop of Reims, had detained the small army at Blois. The old fox had no conception of the irresistible power of enthusiasm; or perhaps he dreaded it. He came at last, with great reluctance. The Maid went out to meet him, with the population and with the priests, all chanting hymns; this procession marched again and again in front of the English bastilles; the army thus entered the city under the protection of clerics and a young girl (May 4, 1429).

The Maid, with all her enthusiasm and her inspiration, was curiously shrewd; she was soon aware that the newcomers were cold toward her, and even hostile. She understood that they meant to act without her, at the risk of compromising everything. As Dunois had admitted to her that they were afraid English reinforcements were on the way, under the command of Sir John Fastolf: "Bastard, bastard," [1] she said to him, "in God's name I charge you to let me know as soon as this Fastolf arrives; for if he comes without my being told, I shall have you beheaded."

She was right in suspecting that they were planning to ignore her. As she was resting for a while by the side of young Charlotte, she stood up suddenly: "Ah! Woe is me!" she cried, "the blood of our men is flowing. . . . It was wickedly done! Why did they not wake me up?" She put on her armor in a moment, and finding her page below, at play: "Ah! cruel boy," she said to him, "why did you not tell me that French blood was being shed!" She went off at a gallop; but soon she met wounded men who were carried back. "Never," said she, "could I see the blood of a Frenchman but my hair would stand on end!"

On her arrival, those who were fleeing turned round. Dunois, who had not been informed either, came about the same time. The bastille (it was one of the northern ones) was attacked once more. Talbot attempted to bring it support. But new forces were sallying forth from Orleans, the Maid placed herself

---

[1] Dunois was the natural son of the duke of Orleans, brother of Charles VI; the term *Bâtard d'Orléans* was commonly used as a title of honor, not as an insult.

at their head, and Talbot ordered his men to retire. The bastille was carried.

Many Englishmen, who had assumed priestly garments in order to escape, were taken over by the Maid and led to her quarters, to ensure their safety; she knew too well how ferocious the fighters on her side could be. It was her first victory, the first time she saw a scene of carnage. She wept at the sight of so many men dying without confession. She wanted to confess, and have her whole retinue do the same; she declared that on the morrow, the Feast of the Ascension, she would take communion and spend the whole day in prayers.

They took advantage of that day. They held a council without her, and they decided that this time they would cross the Loire and attack St. John-the-White, the bastille which offered the greatest obstacle to the bringing in of supplies; and that at the same time an attack would be launched on the other side as a feint. Those who were jealous of the Maid told her only of the feint; but Dunois confessed everything to her.

The English did then what they should have done earlier: they concentrated their forces. They themselves set fire to the bastille which was to be attacked, and retreated to the other two southern bastilles, that of the Augustines and that of the *Tournelles* ("Turrets"). The Augustines was attacked at once, and carried as soon as attacked. This success again was due in part to the Maid. There was a moment of panic among the French, and they swayed back headlong toward the pontoon bridge they had established. The Maid and La Hire extricated themselves from the confused mass, jumped into boats, and launched a flank attack against the English.

The Tournelles alone remained. The victors spent the night before the bastille. But they prevailed upon the Maid, who had eaten nothing that day (it was Friday), to go back across the Loire. In the meantime, the council had assembled. They apprised the Maid in the evening of their unanimous decision: now that the city had been fully revictualed, they would wait for fresh reinforcements before attacking the Tournelles. It is hard to believe that the leaders seriously had any such intention; at any moment, the English might receive support from Fastolf; to procrastinate would be perilous. Probably, what they desired was to deceive the Maid, so as to rob her of all credit for the success she had done so much to prepare. She was not to be caught in the trap.

"You have had your council," she said, "and I have had mine." And turning toward her chaplain: "Come tomorrow at daybreak, and do not leave me. I shall have much to do; my blood will flow; I shall be wounded above the breast."

When morning came, her host attempted to hold her back: "Stay, Joan," he said, "let us eat together this fish which has just been caught."—"Keep it for me," she said gaily; "keep it until this evening, when

I cross the bridge again after capturing the Tournelles; I shall bring with me a *Godden* [2] who will eat his share."

She rode ahead of them, with a crowd of men-at-arms and civilians, as far as the Burgundy Gate. But Squire de Gaucourt, grand master of the king's household, kept it closed. "You are a wicked man," Joan said to him; "whether you like it or not, the men-at-arms shall pass." Gaucourt felt that before such an excited multitude, his life was hanging by a thread; anyway, his own people were no longer following his orders. The crowd opened the gate, and forced another one nearby.

The sun was rising upon the Loire at the time when the confused throng was rushing into boats. However, when they reached the Tournelles, they realized that they needed artillery, and they went back to the city to fetch it. Finally, they attacked the outer bulwark that protected the bastille. The English were fighting valiantly. The Maid, when she saw that the assailants were weakening, jumped into the moat and took hold of a ladder; she was leaning it against the wall when she was struck by an arrow between her neck and her shoulder. The English were sallying forth to capture her; but her own people carried her away. At a distance from the fray, lying

[2] *Godden* or *Godon*, for *God damn*, the only English words the French caught and remembered; so the English were named after their favorite expression. As late as the eve of the French Revolution, Beaumarchais affected to believe that *Goddam* was "the foundation of the English language."

on the grass, her armor removed, she saw how deep was the wound: the point was coming out on the other side; she grew frightened and wept. . . . Suddenly, she stood up; her saints had appeared to her; she sent away the men who thought they could heal the wound with a charm or spell; she had no wish to be cured, she said, against the will of God. She simply allowed them to pour oil on her wound; and she made confession.

Meanwhile, the French were making no progress, and night was at hand. Dunois himself was about to sound the retreat. "Wait a while longer," she said; "drink and eat"; and she began her prayers in a vineyard. A Basque soldier had taken from the Maid's equerry that standard of hers so dreaded by the foe. "As soon as the standard touches the wall," she said, "you will be able to enter."—"It is touching it now." —"Then go in, the position is yours." In fact, the assailants, in a frenzy, went up "as though there had been stairs." The English, at that moment, were being attacked on both sides.

Meanwhile, the people of Orleans, who from the other side of the Loire had been watching the combat, could not restrain themselves any more. They opened the gate and rushed to the bridge. But one of the arches had collapsed; they first threw across the gap a precarious catwalk, and a knight of St. John, in full armor, ventured upon it. The bridge was patched up somehow. The crowd burst out like a flood. The English, when they saw that surging tide of men, thought the whole world was moving upon them. They grew crazy with fear. Some could see St. Aignan, the patron saint of the city; others saw Michael the archangel. Glasdale tried to retreat from the outer bulwark into the bastille over a little bridge; that bridge was shattered by a cannon ball; the English captain fell, and was drowned, under the very eyes of the Maid he had so foully reviled. "Ah!" she said, "I have great pity on thy soul!" There were five hundred men in the bastille: all were put to the sword.

There was not a single Englishman left south of the Loire. The next day, Sunday, those who were still on the north bank abandoned their bastilles, their artillery, their prisoners, their sick. Talbot and Suffolk directed the retreat in good order, and proud to the end. The Maid forbade that they be pursued, since they were retiring of their own accord. Before they were too far away and had lost sight of the city, she had an altar erected in the plain, mass was sung, and the people returned thanks unto the Lord (Sunday, May 8).

The relief of Orleans had a prodigious effect. Everyone saw in it the working of a supernatural power. Some thought it was due to the devil; most believed that it was God's own deed; it became a general opinion that Charles VII had the right on his side.

Six days after the end of the siege, Gerson brought forth and spread abroad a treatise in which he proved that it was legitimate, without any offense to reason, to give God credit for this wonderful event. Good Christine de Pisan wrote also, exulting in the pride of her sex. Several treatises were published, rather favorable than hostile to the Maid; some were composed by subjects of the duke of Burgundy, who was the ally of the English.

The one thing for Charles VII to do was to clutch the opportunity and go forth boldly from Orleans to Reims, there to grasp the crown. This looked like foolhardiness, yet it was easy at that moment when the English were still stricken with amazement and fear. Since through an egregious blunder they had failed to have their young Henry VI crowned, it was urgent to steal a march on them. The first to be anointed would remain the king. It would be a great achievement also for Charles VII to ride in royal state through the part of France held by the English, to affirm possession, to demonstrate that everywhere in France the king was in his own domain.

The Maid alone was of this opinion, and her heroic folly was very wisdom. The shrewd masters of statecraft in the council smiled; they advised moving by steps slow and sure—thus giving the English time to recover from their dismay. Every one of the councilors gave an opinion dictated by self-interest. The duke of Alençon wished the army to move into Normandy, so as to recover Alençon. The others requested—and their advice prevailed—that the royal forces should remain on the Loire, besieging the smaller fortified places; it was the most timid course, and in the interest, above all, of the houses of Orleans and Anjou; it was also the course favored by La Trémouille, who was from Poitou, and Charles VII's favorite.

Suffolk had thrown himself into Jargeau; he was hemmed in there, and the place was stormed. Beaugency also was taken, before Lord Talbot had received from the Regent [3] the aid which Fastolf was bringing. Constable Richemond, who for a long time had remained aloof in his domains, came with his Bretons, against the wishes both of the king and of the Maid: he was hastening to the aid of the victors.

A battle was imminent; Richemond was coming to claim the credit. Talbot and Fastolf had effected their junction; but, strange as it may seem, a good illustration of the condition of the country and of the haphazard character of warfare, the French were unable to locate the English army in the desert of Beauce, at that time covered with copse and bushes. It was a stag that revealed the whereabouts of the enemy: chased by the French vanguard, it rushed into the English ranks.

The English were on the march, so they had not protected themselves with a stockade, as they usually did when camping. Talbot alone wanted to fight it out: his inglorious flight from Orleans rankled in his mind; Sir John Fastolf, on the contrary, who had won

[3] The duke of Bedford, uncle of Henry VI, was regent in France; another uncle, Gloucester, was regent in England.

the battle of the Herrings [4] had no need of a fight to redeem his fame; he said sensibly enough that with a dispirited army it were better to remain on the defensive. The French men-at-arms did not wait for the end of the argument; they came at a gallop, and found little resistance. Talbot fought stubbornly, perhaps seeking death; his valiant efforts only led to his capture. The pursuit was murderous: two thousand English corpses were strewn on the plain. The Maid wept when she saw the carnage, and wept more grievously still when she had to witness the brutal behavior of her soldiers and the ruthless treatment of the prisoners who could not offer ransom; one of them was struck on the head so viciously that he fell mortally wounded; the Maid could not bear the sight, she jumped down from her horse, raised the poor fellow's head, called a priest, comforted him in his last moments.

After this battle of Patay (June 28 or 29), the time had come to venture on the Reims expedition or give it up altogether. The shrewd heads still wanted the army to remain on the Loire, to reduce Cosne and La Charité. This time they spoke in vain: timid voices were no longer listened to. Every day people flocked to the army from all the provinces, roused by the news of the Maid's miracles, putting their faith in her alone, and, like herself, anxious above all for the king

[4] At Rouvray, on February 12, 1429, the French and the Scots attacked Fastolf, who was convoying Lenten provisions, mostly herrings. They were sharply defeated.

to go to Reims. It was an irresistible surge, with the spirit of a pilgrimage and of a crusade. The young king, for all his indolence, allowed himself at last to be carried by that mighty tidal wave of a whole people, which was rising and flowing toward the north. King and courtiers, the cautious and the enthusiastic, pell-mell, willy-nilly, the foolish with the wise, they started on their quest. When they set out they were only twelve thousand; but on the way their numbers grew; more kept coming, and others still; those who had no armor followed the holy expedition as though they were mere *Jacques* or peasants, satisfied, even if they were gentlemen, to fight with plebeian weapons, bows or knives.

The army left Gien on June 28, passed before Auxerre without attempting to enter it: the city was in the hands of the duke of Burgundy, whom they were anxious not to provoke. Troyes had a mixed garrison, Burgundians and Englishmen; when the royal army hove into view, those soldiers sallied forth to challenge it. It was unlikely that such a great city, with such stout defenders, could be stormed without artillery. But how could the army stop to lay a regular siege? How, on the other hand, could the king's forces advance, leaving such a stronghold in its rear? The army was already suffering from hunger. Would it not be better to return to their base in the Loire country? The advocates of caution were triumphing.

There was only one old Armagnac councilor,

President (Judge) Maçon, who took the opposite view, who realized that in such an enterprise wisdom was on the side of enthusiasm, that in a people's crusade cool reason was out of place. "When the king undertook this journey," he said, "it was not because he had a great array of men-at-arms, or a full treasury, or because he thought success possible; he undertook it because Joan was telling him to go ahead, to get himself crowned at Reims; that he would find little resistance, such being God's pleasure."

The Maid, knocking at the door of the council, assured them that within three days they would be able to enter the city. "We would be willing to wait six days," the chancellor said, "if we were sure you were right." "Six days? You will enter tomorrow."

She took up her standard; everyone followed her to the moat; at her command, they threw into it everything they could lay their hands on—faggots, doors, tables, beams. So quick was the work that the people of the city thought that in a trice there would be no moat left. The English, dizzy with fear, began to see strange sights, as they had at Orleans: a swarm of white butterflies fluttering round the magic standard. The burgesses, on their side, were sore afraid; they remembered that it was at Troyes that the treaty had been signed which disinherited Charles VII; they dreaded that the city would be chastised as an example; they were already running to the churches for sanctuary; they were crying that the place should be surrendered. The men-at-arms, nothing loath, agreed to a parley; they were permitted to leave with everything they possessed.

"Everything they possessed" consisted mainly of prisoners—Frenchmen. The councilors of Charles VII, who had drawn up the terms of withdrawal, had failed to make any stipulation in favor of these unfortunate men. The Maid alone thought of their plight. As the English were leaving, taking with them their prisoners in fetters, she went to the gates, and cried out, "Mercy me! They shall not take them away!" And keep them she did, and the king paid their ransom.

Having mastered Troyes on July 9, Charles VII made his entry into Reims on the fifteenth; and on the seventeenth, a Sunday, he was anointed. That very morning the Maid, remembering the precept in the Gospels first to seek reconciliation before offering a sacrifice to the Lord, dictated a noble letter addressed to the duke of Burgundy; she stirred up no tragic memories; she took care that neither side should feel irritated or humiliated, and she said to the duke with tact and dignity, "Forgive each other with your whole heart, as should be done by loyal Christians."

Charles VII was anointed by the archbishop with the chrism kept in the Holy Vial or *ampulla*, which was brought from St. Remy's. He was then, in conformity with the antique ritual, lifted into his seat by the ecclesiastical peers, and waited upon, both during the anointing and during the subsequent banquet, by the secular peers. Then he repaired to St. Marcou's, there to touch the sick for "the king's evil." [5] All the ceremonies were scrupulously performed, not missing a single point. Thus, Charles found himself the true king, the only king, according to the beliefs of the time. The English might now have their Henry VI crowned; this second ceremony could only be, in the minds of the people, a parody of the first.

At the moment when the king was anointed, the Maid threw herself down at his feet and clasped his legs, with a flood of happy tears. The whole congregation was weeping also.

It is asserted that she said to him, "Noble king, now God's will is fulfilled, that I should raise the siege of Orleans, and that I should bring you to your city of Reims, there to receive the Holy Chrism, thus proving that you are the true king, and that the kingdom of France should rightly be yours."

The Maid was right: she had accomplished that which she was appointed to do. So, even amid the joy of this triumphant and solemn ceremony, the thought, perhaps the presentiment of her approaching end, passed through her mind. As she was entering Reims with the king, and as the multitude came out to meet them singing hymns: "Oh! What a good and devout people!" she said. "If I am to die, I should be happy to be buried here." "Joan," the archbishop said, "where

[5] *Ecrouelles*, a form of scrofula. The kings of England, who did not relinquish their claim to the French throne until the end of the seventeenth century, possessed that healing touch; the Stuart pretenders kept it to the end.

do you think you are to die?"—"I know not, where-
ever God pleases . . . I wish it were His pleasure
for me to return home and tend my sheep, with my
sister and my brothers. . . . They would be over-
joyed to see me again! At any rate, I have done what
Our Lord commanded me to do." And she returned
thanks, her eyes lifted up to Heaven. All who saw
her at that moment, an old chronicle reports, believed
more firmly than ever that she had been sent by the
Lord.

III

Joan Betrayed
and Surrendered

Such was the virtue of the anointing and its over-
powering effect in Northern France that from that
time on the expedition seemed but a peaceable af-
firmation of ownership, a triumphal journey, a pro-
longation of the celebration at Reims. The paths
were made smooth before the king, the cities opened
their gates and lowered their drawbridges. The royal
progress was like a pilgrimage from the cathedral of
Reims to the church of St. Medardus at Soissons, to
Notre Dame of Laon. Tarrying a few days in every
city, riding on as he pleased, he entered Château-
Thierry, Provins; thence, well recruited and reposed,
he resumed, in the direction of Picardy, his leisurely
triumph.

Were there any Englishmen left in France? One
might well have doubted it. Since the action at Patay,
no word was heard of Bedford. Not that he was lacking in energy or courage. But he had used up his last

resources. One very significant fact reveals how
straitened were his circumstances: he was no longer
able to pay his court of justice. That court had to
suspend its activities; and when the young king,
Henry VI, entered Paris, the event could not be re-
corded in detail on the registers, as was the custom,
"for lack of parchment."

In such a plight Bedford had no choice. He must
seek the support of the man he loved least, his uncle,
the rich and powerful Cardinal Winchester. But the
latter, avaricious as well as ambitious, kept haggling
in the hope that the delay would bring him still better
terms. The formal agreement was not reached until
the first of July, two days after the battle of Patay.
Meanwhile, Charles VII was entering Troyes and
Reims; Paris was in alarm, and Winchester was still
tarrying in England. Bedford, to defend Paris, called
in the duke of Burgundy. The duke came, but almost
alone; all the advantage the regent could draw from
this visit was to have the duke attend an assembly of
notables, address it, rehearse once again the lamentable story of his father's death. Thereupon the duke
departed, leaving no reinforcement to Bedford except a handful of Picard men-at-arms; and even in
payment for these he exacted the city of Meaux as a
pledge.

Winchester remained Bedford's only hope. This
cleric was the actual sovereign of England. His
nephew, the *Protector* Gloucester, leader of the aris-
tocratic party, had ruined his chances through his

imprudences and his follies. From year to year his
influence in the council had waned; Winchester was
dominant, and reduced the Protector to impotence,
to such a point that every year something was lopped
off his personal appropriation; this was deadly to
Gloucester's influence, in a country where every man
is valued in exact proportion with his resources. Winchester, on the contrary, was the richest of the English princes, and the greatest holder of church
benefices in the world. Power went inevitably with
money. The cardinal and the wealthy bishops of
Canterbury, York, London, Ely, and Bath constituted
the council; if they allowed laymen to attend, it was
on the condition that they would not breathe a word;
and when the meetings were important the laymen
were not even summoned. The English government,
as one might have foreseen as soon as the house of
Lancaster came to the throne, had become entirely
the rule of bishops. This is evident in the documents
of the time. In 1429, the chancellor opened the session
of Parliament with a fierce attack on heresy.

In order to raise the cardinal's power to the highest pitch it was necessary to bring down Bedford in
France as low as Gloucester was in England; he must
be reduced to the point of imploring Wincester's
assistance; whereupon Winchester, at the head of an
army, would come and have the young king Henry
VI anointed. Winchester had this army in readiness;
he had been commissioned by the Pope to lead a crusade against the Hussites of Bohemia, and under this

pretext he had raised a few thousand men. The Pope had granted him the proceeds from the sale of indulgences, to lead his troops into Bohemia; the council of England gave him more money to keep them in France. To their great astonishment, the crusaders discovered that they had been sold by the cardinal; he was paid twice over, paid for an army which he planned to use to make himself king.

With this army, Winchester was to make sure of Paris, bring little Henry VI thither, have him anointed. But that solemn rite would make the cardinal's power secure only if he succeeded in casting discredit on Charles VII's coronation, in dishonoring his victories. Against Charles VII in France, as against Gloucester in England, he proposed to use, as we shall see, the same weapon, a most efficacious one in those days: a trial for witchcraft.

It was on the 25th of July, only nine days after Charles VII had been well and duly anointed, that the cardinal entered Paris with his army. Bedford did not waste a moment; he left at once with his troops to keep watch on Charles VII. Twice the two forces came within fighting range, and there were a few skirmishes. Bedford was in fear of losing Normandy, and he arranged his troops so as to cover that province; in the meantime, the French king was marching on Paris (August).

It was not the Maid's counsel; her voices were telling her not to advance farther than St. Denis. The city where the kings were buried was holy, like the city where they were anointed; beyond that point, she felt obscurely the presence of a power she could not control. Charles VII should have shared that feeling. The countryside had been stirred by the inspiration of holiness under arms, the magic glamour of a crusade: was it not perilous to lead these forces of the spirit against a city of down-to-earth, mocking rationalism, the city of the schoolmen and of the Cabochiens?

It was indeed a foolhardy enterprise. Such a city cannot be captured by a surprise attack; it can be reduced only by cutting off its supplies; but the English had control of the Seine, both above Paris and below. They had strong forces of their own, and they were supported by a number of the inhabitants, who had cast in their lot with the English. Moreover, rumors were spread that the Armagnacs were bent on destroying the city, or razing it to the ground.

The French, however, did carry one outer bulwark. The Maid went down into the first moat; she even cleared the saddle of earth which separated it from the second. Then she discovered that the latter, which surrounded the walls, was filled with water. Indifferent to the hail of arrows, she cried for faggots to be brought, while with her spear she was sounding the depth of the water. She was almost alone, a target for all the bolts; one hit her, and went through her thigh. She tried to overcome the pain, and remained to nerve the troops to the assault. At last, as she was losing much blood, she withdrew to the shelter of the first moat; not until ten or eleven at night could they prevail upon her to retire. She seemed to feel that this flagrant failure, under the very walls of Paris, would irretrievably ruin her position.

Fifteen hundred men were wounded in the action, which she was wrongly accused of having advised. She retired, cursed by her own side as she was by the enemy. She had felt no qualms about ordering the assault on the feast of the Nativity of the Virgin (September 8); the pious city of Paris was greatly scandalized.

The court of Charles VII even more. The libertines, the intriguers, the literalists who hate and despise the spirit, all declared themselves against the spirit at the moment when it appeared to have lost its power. The archbishop of Reims, chancellor of France, who had never been heartily in favor of the Maid, prevailed upon the Council, against Joan's opinion, to open negotiations. He came to Paris to arrange for a truce; perhaps his secret hope was to win over the duke of Burgundy, who at that time was in Paris. Distrusted, ill-supported, the Maid, during that winter, besieged St. Pierre-le-Moûtier and La Charité. At St. Pierre, very nearly abandoned, she still managed to order the assault and capture the city. The siege of La Charité dragged on indefinitely, languished, until a panic terror dispersed the assailants.

In the meantime, the English had secured the determined support of the duke of Burgundy. As he saw them growing weaker, his hopes mounted of keeping for himself the fortified towns he might capture in Picardy. The English, who had just lost Louviers, had to place themselves entirely at his discretion. This prince, the richest in Christendom, no longer hesitated about investing money and men in a war which, he hoped, would turn to his profit. With some gold, he won the governor of Soissons. Then he lay siege to Compiègne, whose governor was likewise a man of dubious integrity. But the inhabitants had too thoroughly committed themselves to the cause of Charles VII to allow their city to be surrendered. The Maid threw herself into it. On the very day of her arrival she headed a sortie, and nearly caught the besiegers by surprise. But in a moment they rallied, and pushed back the defenders as far as the bulwark, as far as the bridge. The Maid had remained in the rear so as to cover the retreat: she was not able to get back into the city in time, either because the fleeing crowd was jamming the bridge, or because the gate had already been closed. Her apparel made her conspicuous; she was quickly surrounded, grabbed at, pulled down from her horse. The man who had taken her, a Picard archer—according to others, it was the Bastard of Vendôme—sold her to John of Luxemburg. All—Englishmen and Burgundians—were amazed to see that this object of terror, this monster, this devil was after all simply a girl of eighteen.

She had known beforehand that such would be her fate; such a cruel destiny was inevitable; and let us dare to say that it was necessary. She had to undergo that suffering. Without the ordeal, and the purification of her last moments, dubious shadows would have remained in the radiance of that holy figure; she would not have stood in the memory of men as THE MAID OF ORLEANS.

She had said, referring to the relief of Orleans and the coronation at Reims, "It is for this I was born." Both these things accomplished, her saintly character was in jeopardy.

War, saintliness, two contradictory terms; it seems that saintliness is the very opposite of war, that it implies charity and peace. But how could a young and valiant heart be engaged in warfare without yielding to the bloodthirsty intoxication of combat and victory? . . . She had said at the outset that she would never use her sword to kill. Later on she spoke with complacency of the sword she carried at Compiègne, "Excellent," she said, "both to thrust and cut." Does not this mark a change? The holy Maid was turning into a captain. The duke of Alençon said that she showed singular aptitude in the handling of the modern weapon, the most murderous, artillery. As the leader of fractious soldiers, constantly grieved and offended by their disorderly conduct, she was becoming harsh and prompt to anger, at least in her efforts to curb them. Above all, she was without mercy for the loose women that the soldiers dragged about with them. One day she struck one of those wretches with the sword of St. Catherine—only with the flat of the blade. But the virgin sword could not bear such a contact; it broke, and no smith could make it whole again.

A short time before she was captured, she herself had made prisoner a Burgundian freebooter, Franquet of Arras, a brigand execrated everywhere in the North. The royal bailiff claimed him, to have him hanged. She refused at first to yield him, with the thought of exchanging him; then she decided to deliver him to the judge. He had a hundred times deserved the gallows; still, that she should surrender a captive, and make herself responsible for a man's death, must have dimmed, even in the eyes of her companions, the halo of her saintliness.

What a misery for such a soul to be enmeshed in the realities of this world! Every day she must have lost something of her integrity. One cannot become rich, honored, the equal of lords and princes, all of a sudden, without having to pay the price. Her handsome garments, the patent of nobility conferred upon her, the favors granted her by the king, all this would undoubtedly, in the long run, have altered her heroic simplicity. She had obtained that her village be exempt from the *taille* (tallage, or poll tax); and the king had made one of her brothers provost of Vaucouleurs.

But the greatest peril for the saintly Maid was her very saintliness, the respect, the worship given her by the common people. At Lagny, they implored her to bring a dead child back to life. The count of

Armagnac asked her in a letter which of the two popes was to be acknowledged.[1] If we are to judge by her letter (which may have been touched up), she had promised to decide at the end of the war, trusting that her inner voices would enable her to pass on the papal authority itself.

Yet it was not pride that moved her. She never gave out that she was a saint; she often admitted that she could not pry into the future. On the eve of a battle she was asked whether the king would be victorious; she replied that she did not know. At Bourges, as some women were beseeching her to touch crosses and rosaries, she merely laughed, and told Dame Margaret, with whom she was staying, "Touch them yourself: it will do just as well."

We repeat that the eminent originality of this young peasant girl was common sense combined with exaltation. It was that very blend, as we shall see, that was to infuriate her judges and make them more implacable. The schoolmen, the logicians, who hated her because she claimed inspiration, were all the more cruel because they could not despise her as a mere lunatic, because, more than once, she invoked a higher reason which silenced their reasoning.

It was not difficult to foresee that she was doomed. She herself was not unaware of it. Right at the beginning she had said, "You must employ me now; I shall

---

[1] From 1378 to 1449, the Church was almost constantly rent by schisms, popes, and antipopes hurling anathemas at one another.

last but one year, or maybe a little over." Many times, addressing her chaplain, Brother Pasquerel, she repeated, "If I am to die soon, tell the king our liege from me that he must establish chapels for people to pray for the souls of those who died in the defense of the kingdom."

When her parents asked her, as they saw her again at Reims, if she were indeed without fear: "I am afraid of nothing," she said, "except treason." Often at dusk, when campaigning, if some church happened to be at hand, particularly one served by the Mendicants, she entered with alacrity, and mingled with the little children who were being instructed for their first communion. If an old chronicle is to be trusted, on the very day she was made prisoner, she went to take communion in the church of St. James' at Compiègne; she leaned, grieving at heart, against one of the pillars, and told the good people and the children who were there in great numbers, "My dear friends, my little children, I tell you for certain that there is a man who has sold me; I have been betrayed, and soon I shall be put to death. Pray for me, I beseech you, for I shall no longer be able to serve my king, and the noble kingdom of France."

It is probable that the Maid was haggled over and bought, in the same fashion as Soissons had just been bought. The English would have given all their gold to lay their hands on her at such a critical moment, just when their young king was landing in France. But the Burgundians wanted her, and they got her; it was in the interest not only of the duke, and of the Burgundian party in general, but specifically of John of Ligny, who at once bought the prisoner.

The Maid had fallen into the hands of a noble lord of the house of Luxemburg, a vassal of the chivalrous duke of Burgundy, whom they called the *good* duke. This was a decisive test of the chivalry of the time. A prisoner of war, a girl, a young girl, and above all a virgin: what could she fear among gentle and loyal knights? Chivalry was in fashion; the defense of dames and maidens in distress was a favorite theme; Marshal Boucicault had just founded an order for that very purpose. Moreover, the worship of the Virgin had been gathering power throughout the Middle Ages; it had become the dominant aspect of religion; and therefore virginity must have appeared as an inviolable safeguard.

To understand what is to follow, we must realize the strange discrepancy that existed in those days between the domain of thought and that of practical life; we must, however shocking the contrast may be, set the sordid realities of the age in opposition to the all-too-sublime ideal embodied in the Maid; we must (I crave the forgiveness of the pure girl whose life I am relating) descend to the lowest circles of a world putrid with greed and lust. If we refused to see that age such as it was, we could not understand how it was possible for knights to barter this living flower of chivalry; how, under the reign of the Virgin, the Virgin appeared only to be so cruelly spurned.

The religion of that time was not so much the Virgin as it was Woman; the ideal of chivalry was that portrayed in *Little John of Saintré;* [2] only the cynical tale was less gross than real life.

The princes set the example. Charles VII entertained Agnès Sorel in the presence of his wife's mother, the old queen of Sicily; mother, wife, paramour, in sweet harmony, he took them all with him on a tour along the Loire.

The English, less flighty, will not seek love except in wedlock; Gloucester properly married Jacqueline; among Jacqueline's ladies-in-waiting he noticed one who was fair and sprightly, so he married her also.

But France and England, in this as in every domain in those days, had to yield precedence to Flanders, to the count of Flanders, the mighty duke of Burgundy. A legend which fitly expresses the spirit of the Low Countries is that of the famous countess who gave birth to three hundred and sixty-five children. The princes of the land, without matching this achievement, strove not to fall too far behind. A count of Clèves had sixty-three bastards. John of Burgundy, bishop of Cambrai, celebrated his pontifical mass attended by his thirty-six bastards or sons of bastards. Philip the Good had only sixteen bastards, but he had no fewer than twenty-seven consorts, three legitimate

---

[2] A tale by Antoine de la Salle, ca. 1456. A page is taught all the refinements of chivalry by an exalted Dame, only to be thrown over in the end for a lusty and brutal monk.

wives, and twenty-four concubines. In those dismal years, 1429 and 1430, while the Maid's tragic fate was being decided, the duke gave himself up without restraint to the joyous affair of his third marriage. This time he was espousing an infanta of Portugal, whose mother was English, Philippa of Lancaster. The English tried to keep the duke with them by giving him the command of Paris; in vain—he was anxious to leave this land of famine, eager to return to Flanders, there to welcome his young bride. Deeds to be engrossed and signed, festivities started, interrupted, taken up again, absorbed month after month. At Bruges in particular, there were incredible feasts, fabulous entertainments, extravagances so crazy that they might ruin the whole nobility; and the burghers were more lavish still. The seventeen nations which had trading centers at Bruges displayed the riches of the entire world. Hanging along the streets were the beautiful and soft carpets of Flanders. For eight days and eight nights, wines kept flowing freely, and of the very best; from a stone lion there poured Rhenish wine, from a stag, the wine of Beaune; a unicorn, at mealtime, spouted rosewater and malmsey.

But the crowning splendor of the Flemish festival was the triumphal beauty of the Bruges women, such types as Rubens was to paint, for example the Magdalen of his *Descent from the Cross*. The Portuguese bride cannot have met her new subjects with unalloyed pleasure. Already the Spanish princess, Joanna of Navarre, put out of humor at the sight of such luxury, had blurted out, "I see none but queens in this place."

On his wedding day (January 10, 1430), Philip the Good instituted the order of the Golden Fleece "conquered by Jason." To reassure his wife, he adopted the device: "None other shall I have."

Did the bride trust such a promise? It may well be doubted. This "fleece" of Jason's (or, as the Church hastened to rebaptize it, this fleece of Gideon's) was after all a Golden Fleece; it evoked those waves of gold, that streaming wealth of golden hair, which Van Eyck, the famous court painter of Philip the Good, lovingly spread over the shoulders of his holy women. Everyone saw in the new order the apotheosis of blond beauty, the youthful luscious beauty of the North, in despite of the South's dark beauties. It seemed as though the Flemish prince, in order to comfort the women of Flanders, were addressing to *them* the wilfully ambiguous words, "None other shall I have."

Under these chivalric forms, a clumsy pastiching of the knightly romances, the history of Flanders in those days was like a lusty *kermesse,* a riotous fair, joyous and sensual. Tournaments, passages-at-arms, banquets of the Round Table, all served merely as pretexts for gallant encounters, for easy and vulgar love affairs, for interminable bouts of gluttony. The true device of the time is the one the Squire of Ternant dared to adopt for the jousts at Arras: "May my desires be sated, and I crave no other boon!"

The surprising fact was that in the midst of these

crazy festivities, these ruinous displays of magnificence, the affairs of the count of Flanders seemed all
the more flourishing. Give away, lose, waste his wealth
as he might, more and still more kept accruing to him.
His power was growing, his possessions extending,
in the midst of universal ruin. Only Holland offered
a check; but he acquired with little trouble the positions that controlled the Somme and the Meuse,
Péronne, Namur. In addition to Péronne, the English
handed over to him Bar-on-the-Seine, Auxerre, Meaux,
all the roads into Paris, and at last Paris itself.

Luck upon luck; fortune went loading and over-
loading him with its favors. He no longer had time
to breathe. It was fortune that put the Maid in the
clutches of one of his vassals—the Maid, that priceless
hostage whom the English would have been eager to
buy at any cost. And at the same time, a new piece of
good luck added to the intricacy of his situation: the
succession of Brabant was opened. But he could not
get the benefit of it unless he could make sure of
England's good will.

The duke of Brabant had been talking of marry-
ing again, of begetting heirs of his own loins. He died
just at the right time for the duke of Burgundy. The
latter owned practically everything that surrounds
Brabant—I mean Flanders, Hainaut, Holland, Namur,
Luxemburg. Nothing was lacking but the central
province, Louvain, a city of wealth, and Brussels, a
seat of power. Strong was the temptation. So the duke
paid no regard to the rights of his aunt, Margaret of

Burgundy, although it was from her that his own claims derived; he sacrificed in the same way the rights of his wards, his own honor, his integrity as a guardian. He grabbed Brabant. To hold it, to finish off his difficulties with Holland and Luxemburg, to drive back the people of Liège who were advancing to besiege Namur, it was essential for him to remain on good terms with the English; and that meant turning the Maid over to them.

Philip the *Good* was a kindly man, according to the common conception of kindness; he was tender-hearted, especially with women; a good son; a good father; and always ready to weep. He wept over the men who died at Agincourt; but his alliance with England caused more deaths than Agincourt. He shed torrents of tears on the death of his father; then, to avenge him, he shed torrents of blood. Sentimentality, sensuality: the two often go hand in hand. But sensuality, lust, easily become cruel when occasion arises. Let the coveted object withdraw, let concupiscence watch it flee and elude its clutches, then lust turns into blind fury. Woe to whatever obstacle stands in the way! Rubens and his school, in their pictures of pagan bacchanalia, liked to paint tigers mingled with the satyrs. *"Lust hard by hate."* [3]

The man into whose hands Joan had fallen, John of Ligny, vassal of the duke of Burgundy, happened to be in the same situation as his overlord. He too was sorely tempted by his cupidity. He belonged to

[3] Milton, *Paradise Lost*, I, 417.

the noble house of Luxemburg; because he had the honor of kinship with the Emperor Henry VII and with king John of Bohemia, he had to be treated with consideration; but John of Ligny was poor; he was the younger son of a younger son. He had contrived to be appointed the sole legatee of his aunt, the rich Lady of Ligny and St. Pol. This act of favoritism was very questionable; and it was to be disputed by his elder brother. While in this uncertainty, John was the docile and trembling servant of the duke of Burgundy, of the English, of everybody. The English were urging him to deliver the prisoner into their keeping; it would have been easy for them to seize her in the tower of Beaulieu, where John of Ligny had confined her. On the other hand, if he allowed her to be taken, he would offend the duke of Burgundy, his suzerain, his judge in the matter of the contested inheritance—able therefore to ruin him with a single word. Provisionally, he sent Joan to his castle of Beaurevoir, near Cambrai, in imperial territory.

The English, frantic with hatred and humiliation, were pressing and threatening him. Such was their rage against the Maid that they had a woman burnt alive, simply for having spoken well of her. If the Maid herself were not brought to judgment and burnt as a witch, if her victories were not ascribed to the devil, they would stand in the popular mind as miracles, as works of God; this would show that God was against the English, that their defeat had been beyond doubt and well deserved; therefore their cause was that of the devil; in the opinion of the time, there was no middle ground. Such a conclusion, which English pride found intolerable, was all the more offensive for a government dominated by bishops, as was the case in England; offensive above all for the cardinal, who was its mastermind.

Winchester had taken hold of affairs at a moment when they had reached an almost desperate strait. Gloucester had been reduced to a cipher in England, Bedford in France: Winchester found himself alone. He had thought he would rally and rouse those on the English side by bringing the young king to Calais (April 23), but the English did not stir. He tried to challenge their pride by issuing an ordinance "against those who were afraid of the Maid's magic spells." It had no effect. The king remained at Calais like a stranded vessel. Winchester was becoming ridiculous. After having reduced his crusade to the Holy Land to one against Bohemia, he had to restrict himself to a crusade to save Paris. The bellicose prelate, who had boasted of entering Notre Dame as a conqueror, and having his ward anointed there, found every road closed against him; from Compiègne, the enemy barred the Picardy road; from Louviers, the Normandy highway. In the meantime, the war was dragging on, money was running to waste, the crusade was going up in smoke. Evidently the devil had a hand in all this; the cardinal could extricate himself only by bringing the Evil One himself to judgment, by burning this devil-spawned Maid.

But first he must get hold of her, wrest her from the keeping of the Burgundians. She had been taken on May 23; on May 26, a message was sent from Rouen in the name of the vicar of the Inquisition, requesting the duke of Burgundy and John of Ligny to surrender this woman, suspected of witchcraft. The Inquisition had no great power in France; its vicar was a monk, a very timorous man, a Dominican, and probably, like the rest of the Mendicants, at heart in favor of the Maid. But he lived at Rouen in constant terror of the all-powerful cardinal, who urged him on relentlessly. The cardinal had just appointed as captain of Rouen a man of action thoroughly under his control, Lord Warwick, the guardian of Henry VI. Warwick thus held two commissions, extremely different, both indicative of his master's unquestioning trust—the keeping of the king and that of the king's enemy; the education of the young prince, the supervision of the Maid's trial.

The letter from the monk had little weight: the English secured at the same time a letter from the University of Paris. It seemed rather difficult for the University men heartily to endorse a trial under the Pope's Inquisition, at the moment when, at the Council of Basel, they were intending to oppose the Pope on behalf of the episcopate. Winchester himself, as the head of the English hierarchy, would naturally have preferred a trial conducted by bishops; or, if it could be managed, one in which bishops and Inquisition would work together. Now, he just chanced to have

with him, in his retinue, a bishop admirably fitted
for the task; a beggarly bishop, who was fed at his
board, and who could be relied upon to swear and to
pass sentence exactly as needed.

Peter Cauchon, bishop of Beauvais, was not
devoid of merit. Born at Reims, close to Gerson's
birthplace, he was a very influential doctor in the
University, a friend of Clémengis, who assures us
that he was "kindly and charitable." This kindness of
heart had not prevented him from being among the
most violent in the violent party of the Cabochiens.
This led to his expulsion from Paris in 1413. He returned with the duke of Burgundy, was made bishop
of Beauvais, and under English rule, was elected by
the University as the defender of its privileges. But
the invasion of Northern France by Charles VII in
1429 was a disaster for Cauchon; he attempted to
keep Beauvais for the English party, and was driven
out by the inhabitants. He did not waste his time in
Paris with the lamentable Bedford, who was unable
to reward zealous service; he went straight where
wealth and power were to be found, in England, with
Cardinal Winchester. He became English, he took to
speaking English. Winchester realized what use he
could make of such a man; he attached him to his
fortune by doing for him as much as Cauchon could
ever have hoped, and more. The archbishop of Rouen
had just been moved to another see; Winchester rec-
ommended Cauchon for that high dignity. But
neither the Pope nor the chapter wanted Cauchon;

Rouen was at that time at war with the University of
Paris, and could not accept as its archbishop a man
who belonged to that body. The whole affair remained in suspense; Cauchon, with this magnificent
prey dangling before his eyes, stood gaping, obstinately hoping that the invincible cardinal would sweep
aside all obstacles; wholeheartedly devoted to his
patron, the bishop had no other God.

Most opportunely it happened that the Maid had
been captured near the boundary of Cauchon's diocese; not actually within the diocese, but it was hoped
that people would easily be deluded on that point.
As judge-in-ordinary, Cauchon then wrote to the
king of England to claim jurisdiction; and on June
12, a letter royal notified the University that the
bishop and the inquisitor would sit as judges jointly
and concurrently. The procedure of the Inquisition
differed from that of the episcopal courts. Yet no
objection was raised. Since the two justices were
thus willing to overlook this difficulty, there remained
but one obstacle: the accused was still in the hands
of the Burgundians.

The University took the initiative: it wrote
another message to the duke of Burgundy and to John
of Ligny (July 14). Cauchon, in his eagerness to act
as the agent, as the courier, of the English, took it upon
himself to deliver the letter personally; and he handed
it to the two dukes. At the same time, he enjoined
them to deliver into his hands a prisoner over whom
he had jurisdiction. In these strange dealings, he was

passing from the role of a judge to that of a negotiator, and offered money; although this woman could not be considered as a war prisoner, the king of England, to get her, would give two or three hundred pounds a year to the Bastard of Vendôme; and to those who were actually holding her, a sum of six thousand pounds. Then, toward the end of the letter, Cauchon raised the offer to ten thousand francs, and pointed out that this was a most handsome proposal: "As much," he said, "as would be given for a king or a prince, according to the custom of France."

The English did not rely altogether upon the various steps taken by the University and by Cauchon: they used more drastic means. On the very day Cauchon presented his summons, or on the next, the council of England forbade English merchants to trade in the markets of the Low Countries (July 19), and specifically in that of Antwerp; they were ordered not to purchase linen there, or any of the other articles they used to get in exchange for their wool. This was a shrewd blow aimed at the duke of Burgundy, count of Flanders; it would cripple the two major industries of the Flemings, linen and woolen cloth; the English would no longer buy the former, nor provide the raw material for the latter.

While the English were making such efforts to destroy the Maid, was Charles VII doing anything to save her? Not a thing, it appears; yet he held war prisoners; he could have protected her with the threat of reprisals. Not long before, he had negotiated with his enemies through his chancellor, the archbishop of Reims; but the archbishop and the other "realists" had never been wholeheartedly in favor of the Maid. The Anjou-Lorraine party, with the old queen of Sicily, who had received Joan with enthusiasm, were now unable to intercede in her favor with the duke of Burgundy. The duke of Lorraine was at the point of death; his succession was already hotly disputed; René of Anjou, his son-in-law, expected to be his heir; but against him Philip the Good was supporting a competitor.

Thus on every side this world of selfish interests and greed was arrayed against the Maid, or at least indifferent to her fate. Good Charles VII did nothing for her; good Philip of Burgundy handed her over to her enemies. The house of Anjou wanted Lorraine, the duke of Burgundy wanted Brabant; most of all he wanted the trade of Flanders with England to continue. The minor characters in this drama likewise had their selfish hopes: John of Ligny was coveting the heritage of St. Pol, Cauchon the archbishopric of Rouen.

In vain did John of Ligny's wife cast herself at his feet; in vain did she plead with him not to dishonor himself. He was not free; he had already received English gold; he surrendered Joan not, however, directly to the English, but to the duke of Burgundy. The family of Ligny and St. Pol, with its memories of grandeur and its boundless ambitions, was to pursue its dream of fortune to the very end,

to the Grève.[4] The man who surrendered the Maid
seems to have felt his wretched impotence; he caused
to be painted on his coat of arms a camel staggering
under its load, with a melancholy device that all
courageous men would spurn: "No one is bound to
attempt the impossible."

[4] The *Grève* was the central square in Paris, on the banks
of the Seine, where criminals were executed. An allusion to
John of Ligny's nephew, Constable St. Pol, later beheaded
there in 1475.

IV

The Trial
Joan Refuses to Submit

In the meantime, what of the prisoner? Her body was at Beaurevoir; her soul at Compiègne. In her mind she was still fighting with all her heart for the king who was abandoning her. She felt that without her the loyal city of Compiègne would succumb, and with it the king's cause throughout Northern France. Once already she had tried to escape from the tower at Beaulieu. At Beaurevoir, she was even more strongly tempted to flee; she knew that the English were demanding her; she was horror-stricken at the thought of falling into their hands. She consulted her saints and received no answer from them, except that she must be ready to suffer, "that she would not be delivered until she had seen the king of the English." "But," she said in her heart, "will God allow the poor people of Compiègne to perish?" Under the guise of ardent compassion, temptation conquered. In spite of all that her saints could say, she refused for the

first time to follow their guidance; she threw herself
down from the tower, and fell to the ground half
dead. She was lifted up, nursed by the ladies of the
Ligny household; but she wanted to die, and for two
days she refused to eat.

Surrendered to the duke of Burgundy, she was
taken to Arras, thence to the keep of Le Crotoy, the
ruins of which have now disappeared under the sands.
There she could catch glimpses of the sea, and at times
she could discern the cliffs of England, the land of
the enemy, into which she had hoped to carry the
war and deliver the duke of Orleans. Every morning
a priest who was likewise a prisoner said mass in the
tower. Joan prayed ardently, and her petitions were
heard. Although a captive, she was not without power;
so long as she was alive, her prayers pierced the walls
and pushed back the foe.

On the very day she had foretold, according to
a revelation from the archangel, on November 1,
Compiègne was relieved. The duke of Burgundy had
advanced as far as Noyon, as if to suffer the rebuff
at closer range and in his own person. He was defeated
again a short while later at Germigny (November
20). At Péronne, Saintrailles challenged him to battle,
but he shrank from the test.

These humiliations confirmed the duke in his
alliance with the English and decided him to turn
Joan over to them. But the mere threat of a commer-
cial embargo would have sufficed. The count of
Flanders fancied himself as a knight and the restorer

of the knightly spirit; but in truth he was only the agent of craftsmen and merchants. The cities which wove cloth and the countryside where flax was spun would not patiently have accepted the interruption of their trade and the unemployment it would entail; a revolt would have broken out.

At the moment when the English got hold of the Maid at last, their affairs were in a sorry plight. Not only had they failed to recapture Louviers, but they had lost Châteaugaillard; La Hire took the great fortress by storm; there he found Barbazan a prisoner, and he set that redoubtable captain free. The cities, of their own accord, were going over to Charles VII; the burghers drove out the English. Those of Meaux, so near Paris, chased away their English garrison.

To check this rapid decline of the English cause —if it were possible at all—a great and powerful instrument was needed. Winchester possessed one that he could bring into action: the trial of the Maid, the coronation of his king. The two were to act together, or rather they were one and the same; if he could cast dishonor on Charles VII, prove that he had been led to his anointing by a witch, then the coronation of Henry VI would acquire a halo of sanctification; if one claimant were exposed as the devil's anointed, the other would appear as the Lord's.

Henry entered Paris on December 2. As early as November 21, the University had been induced to write Cauchon, and tax him with slackness; the king was respectfully urged to open the trial. Cauchon was in no hurry; he was reluctant to start the work while the reward remained uncertain. It was only a month later that he secured from the chapter of Rouen Cathedral permission to prosecute in its diocese. There-upon (January 3, 1431) Winchester issued an ordi-nance in which the king was made to say that "on the request of the bishop of Beauvais, and exhorted by his beloved daughter the University of Paris, he com-manded the keepers to *bring* the accused to the bishop." To bring, not to surrender: she was only loaned to the ecclesiastical judge; "reserving the right to take her back again in case she were not convicted." The English ran no risk; she could not escape death; if fire failed, steel would remain.

On January 9, 1431, Cauchon opened the trial at Rouen. He had the vicar of the Inquisition take a seat by his side; and he started with a sort of con-sultation with eight doctors, licentiates or masters of arts of Rouen. He put before them the information he had collected about the Maid. This information, gathered in advance by the enemies of the accused, did not appear substantial enough to the legal minds of the Rouen experts; so flimsy was it that the accusa-tion, which on these faulty data had been *witchcraft*, had to be changed to *heresy*.

Cauchon, to win over those fractious Normans, to allay their superstitious scruples about the niceties of procedure, appointed one of them, John de la Fon-taine, as examining councilor. But he reserved the most active part, that of promoter of the trial, a sort of prosecuting attorney, for a certain Estivet, one of his canons at Beauvais, who had followed him. With all these preliminaries, he managed to waste a whole month; but at last, after the young king had been taken back to London (February 9), Winchester, no longer having to worry on that score, swiftly turned his attention to the trial; he thought, rightly enough, that things are more efficiently done under the master's own eyes; he established himself at Rouen, so as to watch how Cauchon would proceed.

The first step was to win over the monk who was the representative of the Inquisition. Cauchon, having assembled all his assistants, Norman priests and doctors from Paris, in the house of a canon, summoned the Inquisitor and called upon him to act as his associate. The monk answered that "if his powers were found adequate, he would do the proper thing." The bishop assured him that his powers were ample. But the monk went on objecting "that he would much prefer to abstain, both in consideration of his own scruples, and to make sure that the trial would be above challenge." He suggested that the bishop should appoint somebody else, until he, the monk, were absolutely convinced that his powers were sufficient.

He argued and pleaded in vain: he could not escape; willy-nilly, he had to be a judge. One thing besides his timorousness no doubt contributed to his remaining on the bench: Winchester had twenty golden *sous* allocated to him for his trouble. The mendicant had probably never seen so much gold in his whole life.

On February 21 the Maid was brought before her judges. The bishop of Beauvais admonished her "with gentleness and charity," urging her to answer truthfully any question she might be asked, so as to shorten the trial and unburden her conscience, without subterfuges. *Answer:* "I do not know what you propose to question me about; you might ask me things which I would not tell you." She agreed to swear that she would tell the truth about anything not connected with her visions: "But on that last point," she said, "you'd have to cut off my head first." However, she was prevailed upon to swear that she would answer "on anything concerning the faith."

She was urged again on the following day, February 22, and once more on February 24, to pledge herself unconditionally. She was still resisting: "Even little children repeat *that oftentimes people are hanged for having told the truth.*" In weariness, she finally agreed that she would tell everything she knew if it had a bearing on her trial; but not everything she knew.

Questioned about her age, her name, and the name by which she was commonly known, she said she was about nineteen. "In my native place, they used to call me Jehannette; in France, Jehanne. . . ." As for the term the people used, *the Maid*, it seems that a quirk of feminine modesty made her reluctant to mention it; she eluded the difficulty with a white lie: "As to what they call me, I know nothing about it."

She complained that she had been fettered. The bishop said that since she had repeatedly attempted to escape, it had been necessary to shackle her. "It is true," she said; "I have tried. Any prisoner has the right to do so. If I did escape, no one could accuse me of having broken faith; for I have promised nothing."

They ordered her to recite the *Pater Noster* and the *Ave Maria*, perhaps in the superstitious belief that if she were a thrall of the devil, she would not be able to repeat these prayers. "I shall be glad to say them, if only my Lord the bishop of Beauvais consents to hear me in confession." A clever and touching request; by this offer to take her judge, her enemy, into her fullest confidence, she would have made him her father in the spirit and compelled him to bear witness to her innocence.

Cauchon refused; but I am inclined to believe that he was not unmoved. He adjourned the session for the day; on the morrow, he did not question her himself, but turned the task over to one of his assessors.

At the fourth session, a strange quickening of her spirits was manifest. She did not conceal that she had heard her voices: "They woke me up," she said. "I folded my hands and begged of them to advise me;

they said to me: Ask Our Lord."—"And what else did they say?"—"That I should answer you without fear."

"I am not free to speak everything out; I dread far more to offend them than I am afraid of answering you. . . . This day I beg of you not to question me."

The bishop insisted, aware that she was deeply stirred: "But, Joan, is it then possible to offend God by telling what is true?"—"My voices have told me certain things that were not meant for you, but for the king." And she added with eager wistfulness: "Ah! If he could know them, he would enjoy his meat in greater ease . . . I wish he could know them, even if I were to have no wine until Easter."

Mingled with such naïve sayings, there were sublime utterances. "I was sent by God; I have naught to do here; send me back to God, from Whom I came. . . ."

"You tell me you are my judge; ponder with great care over what you mean to do, for in very truth I was sent of God, and you are putting yourself in great jeopardy."

These words must have irritated the judges, and they asked her an insidious and perfidious question, such a question that it is sinful to ask of any living human creature: "Joan, do you believe that you are in a state of grace?"

They thought they had her caught in a snare that nothing could loosen. If she said *No*, she confessed herself unworthy to be God's instrument. But on the other hand, how could she say *Yes?* Who among us frail creatures is certain here below to be indeed in the grace of God? No one except the proud and the presumptuous, the very ones who are farthest from grace.

She cut the knot with heroic and Christian simplicity: "If I am not, may it please God to bring me into it; if I am, may He preserve me in it."

The pharisees were dumfounded.

But for all her heroism, she was a woman still. . . . After these sublime words, she relapsed, she grew softer, she doubted her state, as is natural for a Christian soul, she probed herself, she strove to reassure herself: "Ah! If I knew I was not in God's grace, no one in the world could be more afflicted. . . . But if I were in a state of sin, surely the voices would not come to me . . . I wish everyone could hear them as I do. . . ."

These words gave the judges a weapon against her. After a long pause, they attacked her anew, with fiercer hatred, and they asked her in quick succession questions which might have led to her undoing. Did not the voices tell her to *hate* the Burgundians? . . . Did she not go, as a child, to the tree of the fairies? Etc. They would have liked forthwith to have her burnt as a witch.

At the fifth session she was attacked on a delicate, a perilous point, that of the apparitions. The bishop, suddenly turning all honeyed compassion, had this question put to her: "Joan, how have you been since last Saturday?"—"You may see for yourself," the poor shackled prisoner answered, "I have been as well as I could."

"Joan, are you fasting every day in this Lenten season?"—"Is that part of the trial?"—"Yes indeed" —"Well then, I have kept my fast."

She was then examined searchingly about her visions, about a sign said to have appeared to the dauphin, about St. Catherine and St. Michael. Among other hostile and unseemly questions, she was asked whether St. Michael, when he appeared to her, *was naked?* . . . She answered this question, not even aware of its nastiness, with heavenly purity: "Do you think Our Lord did not have the wherewithal to clothe him?"

On the third of March, there were other bizarre questions, intended to make her confess to some devil's work, to some ugly familiarity with the fiend. "This St. Michael, these sainted women, did they have a body, limbs? The figures you saw, were they angels indeed?"—"Yes, I believe it as firmly as I believe in God." This answer was carefully noted down.

Then they went on to the man's garments she wore, to her standard. "Did not the men-at-arms get standards made after the pattern of yours? Did they not renew them?"—"Yes, when the staff got broken." —"Did you not tell them that these standards would bring them luck?"—"No, I simply told them: 'Fall boldly upon the English,' and I did so myself."

"But why was this standard carried into the

church at Reims for the king's anointing, rather than those of the other captains?"—"It had seen all the dangers; it was meet it should share the honors."

"What was in people's minds when they kissed your feet, your hands, your garments?"—"The poor came to me gladly, because I never did them any hurt; I helped them and protected them as much as I was able."

No man's heart but was touched by answers such as these. Cauchon thought it more prudent to proceed with only a few men he could trust, and as quietly as possible. Since the beginning of the trial, we find the number of the assessors present varying from session to session; some left, others came. The place also varied: the accused at first was questioned in the hall of the castle of Rouen, later in her prison. Cauchon, "not to bother the others," went there with only two assessors and two witnesses (March 10–17). What may have emboldened him thus to proceed in secret session was that he was now sure the Inquisition was supporting him; the vicar had at last received from the inquisitor general for France due authority to judge jointly with the bishop (March 12).

In these fresh examinations they pressed her only on a few points, which Cauchon had indicated in advance.

Had the voices commanded the sally from Compiègne which led to her capture? She did not give a direct answer: "The saints had indeed told me that I was to be taken before the feast of St. John; that this was necessary; that I must not be astonished, but must willingly submit to everything, and that God would come to my aid. . . . Since it was God's pleasure, it was meet that I should be taken."

"Do you believe you did rightly in leaving your parents without their permission? Should not one's father and mother be honored?"—"They have forgiven me."—"Then you thought it was no sin?"— "God had commanded: not for a hundred fathers and a hundred mothers would I have stayed behind."

"Did not the voices call you daughter of God, daughter of the Church, great-hearted Maid?"— "Before the siege of Orleans was raised, and since, the voices called me, and are still calling me every day: Joan the Maid, daughter of God."

"Was it right for you to attack Paris on the day of the Nativity of Our Lady?"—"It is right to observe the feasts of Our Lady; it were well, in good conscience, if we kept them every day."

"Why did you jump from the tower of Beaurevoir?" (They wanted her to confess that she had tried to kill herself.) "I heard that the poor people of Compiègne would all be put to death, even children of seven; besides, I knew I had been sold to the English; I should have preferred to die rather than be in the hands of the English."

"Do St. Catherine and St. Margaret hate the English?"—"They love those whom Our Lord loves, and hate those whom He hates."—"Does God hate the

English?"—"Whether He loves them or hates them, and what He proposes to do with their souls I know not; but this I know for certain, that all of them will be thrown out of France, except those who perish there."

"Is it not a mortal sin to hold a man to ransom, and then to have him killed?"—"I have never done that."—"Was not Franquet of Arras put to death?" —"I consented to it, because I was not able to have him exchanged for one of my men; he confessed he was a brigand and a traitor. His trial went on for a fortnight before the bailiff's court at Senlis."—"Did you not give money to the man who had taken Franquet?"—"I am not the Treasurer of France that I should give out money."

"Do you believe your king was right in killing or causing to be killed the duke of Burgundy?"—"It was most harmful to the kingdom of France. But whatever quarrel there was between them, God sent me to the aid of the king of France."

"Joan, has it been revealed to you that you would escape?"—"This has no bearing on the trial. Do you want me to testify against myself?"—"Have the voices told you nothing on that point?"—"This has nothing to do with the trial; I leave it all in the hands of Our Lord, Who will act according to His pleasure. . . ." And after a silence: "By my faith! I know neither the day nor the hour. God's will be done."— "Then your voices have given you no light, not even in a general way?"—"Well, yes; they tell me that I would be delivered, that I should be of good cheer and courage. . . ."

Another day, she added: "The saints tell me that I shall be delivered with a great victory; and again they tell me: 'Accept everything with a willing heart; be not dismayed at the thought of martyrdom; for it will lead you at last to the kingdom of Heaven.'" —"And since they told you that, you are assured that you are saved and that you will not go to hell?"—"Yes, I believe what they told me as firmly as if I were saved already."—"This answer is of great consequence."—"Yes, to me this is a great treasure."—"So you believe that you no longer could commit a mortal sin?"—"I know not: I leave it all in the hands of Our Lord."

At last the judges had reached the proper ground for the accusation; now they had her in their power. To convict this pure and holy Maid of witchcraft was preposterous; that indictment had to be abandoned; but in her very saintliness, as in that of all the mystics, there was a point which could easily be attacked: the secret voice held equal to, or even placed above, the teachings of the Church, the commands of authority; inspiration, but free; revelation, but personal; submission to God, but what God? The God within.

They closed these preliminary examinations by asking her whether she would let the Church be the final judge of everything she had said and done. To

this she replied: "I love the Church, and I want to up-
hold her with all my strength. As to the good works I
have wrought, I must refer them to the King of
Heaven, Who sent me."

When the question was repeated, she gave no
other answer, but added: "The Church and the Lord
are one."

They told her that a distinction should be made;
that there was the Church *triumphant*, God, the saints,
the souls that had been saved, and the Church *militant*,
the pope, the cardinals, all good Christians; that
Church, "properly assembled," could not err and
was guided by the Holy Ghost. "Will you then submit to the Church *militant?*"—"I came to the king of
France sent by God, by the Virgin, by the saints and
the Church *victorious* above: to *that* Church do I
submit myself, my works, all I have done, all I have
still to do."—"And to the Church *militant?*"—"I shall
answer nothing further at this time."

If we were to believe one of the assessors, she
said that, on certain points, she would take no one's
word, no, neither pope's nor bishops'; what she knew,
she had from God.

The problem of the trial was thus posed in all
its simplicity and its grandeur; the essential debate
opened: on the one hand, the visible Church and established authority, on the other, inspiration seeking
its warrant in the Church invisible. . . . Invisible to
the eyes of the vulgar, but the pious girl saw it plainly,
contemplated it unceasingly, heard it within herself;

she carried the holy women and the angels in her heart. . . . There, for her, was the Church, there was God's radiance: everywhere else, how dim He remained!

Such being the issue, there was no remedy: the accused was bound to destroy herself. She could not yield, she could not, without lying, repudiate, deny that which she saw and heard so distinctly. On the other hand (it might be said), could authority remain an authority, if it abdicated, abandoned its jurisdiction, failed to punish? The Church militant is a church bearing arms, a church wielding the two-edged sword. Against whom? Apparently against all who refuse to obey.

Terrible indeed was that Church in the persons of logicians, schoolmen, enemies of personal inspiration; terrible and implacable when represented by the bishop of Beauvais. But above the bishop, were there no other judges? The party of the bishops and of the University was upholding the supremacy of the councils: was it not bound to recognize as the final judge, in this particular case, its own Council of Basel, which was just about to open? On the other hand, the papal Inquisition, the Dominican who was its vicar, could not dispute that the pope's jurisdiction was superior to their own, which emanated from it.

A *legist*, or expert in the law, at Rouen, that same John de la Fontaine who was a friend of Cauchon and hostile to the Maid, found himself in conscience bound to inform the accused—who had no counsel—that there were judges in appeal; and that, without sacrificing anything in her plea, she could have recourse to them. Two monks opined that the supreme right of the pope should be explicitly reserved.

However irregular it might be for assessors to visit the accused individually, and advise her, these honest men, who saw all the forms violated by Cauchon in the interest of iniquity, did not hesitate to violate them in their turn in the interest of justice. They went fearlessly to the prison, demanded admission, and advised Joan to appeal. The next day, she did appeal to the pope and to the council. Cauchon, incensed, summoned the guards and asked them who had visited the Maid. The legist and the two monks were in actual peril of their lives. From that day, they disappeared; and with them the last semblance of a judicially conducted trial.

Cauchon had hoped at first to win over the legal experts, whose authority was so great in Rouen. But he had soon discovered that he would have to do without them. When he communicated the first minutes of the trial to one of these sober-minded jurists, Master John Lohier, the latter answered definitely that everything about the trial was wrong; that it failed to respect the proper forms; that the assessors were not free; that the sessions were held in secrecy; that the accused, an untaught peasant girl, could not be expected to answer about such weighty matters and to argue with learned doctors. Finally, the man of the Law dared to tell the man of the Church: "This is a trial to impugn the honor of the prince whose cause this girl is supporting; you should frankly say so, and you should have a counsel appointed for her." This attitude of fearless dignity, which reminds us of Papinian's before Caracalla, might have been fraught with disaster for Lohier. But the Norman Papinian did not wait for death in his curule chair: he left at once for Rome.

It seems that Cauchon would get better support from the theologians. After the first examinations, armed with the answers that could be used against the Maid, he closeted himself with his intimate associates; and, relying mainly on the skillful pen of a member of the University of Paris, he drew from those answers a small number of articles upon which the most noted doctors and the ecclesiastical bodies would be requested to express an opinion. This was a detestable custom, but (although this has been disputed) it was the established and regular custom in Inquisition trials. The propositions extracted from the answers of the Maid, and written up as if they were general affirmations, offered a deceitful appearance of impartiality. As a matter of fact, they were a travesty of her answers; and they could not fail to be condemned by the doctors called in consultation; thus serving the hostile intent of the iniquitous man who had framed them.

But, in spite of the tendentious twist in the text, in spite of the terror which weighed upon the doctors, their answers were not unanimously against the accused. Among the doctors, those who were in truth sound theologians and earnest believers, those who had preserved the unwavering faith of the Middle Ages could not so easily reject apparitions and visions. To do so would be casting doubt on all the marvelous happenings reported of the saints; it would have been a challenge to all the legends. The venerable bishop of Avranches, whom they went to consult, answered that according to the doctrines of St. Thomas there was nothing incredible in what the girl asserted, nothing that could be lightly dismissed.

The bishop of Lisieux, admitting that the revelations made to Joan might have been dictated by the devil, added that on the human plane they might be purely and simply *lies* and that if Joan refused to submit to the Church she must be considered as schismatic and her faith must be viewed with the most grievous *suspicion.*

Several legists answered with the Norman gift for subtle equivocation, that she must be held guilty, and most guilty, *unless she were acting under God's orders.* A bachelor went farther; while condemning her, he proposed that, in consideration of the frailty of her sex, *the twelve propositions be repeated to her* (he rightly suspected that they had not been communicated to her); and this done, that the propositions be submitted to the pope. This would have meant an indefinite adjournment.

The assessors, assembled in the chapel of the archbishop's palace, had decided against the Maid in the matter of the twelve propositions. The chapter of Rouen, also consulted, was in no hurry to decide and to assure the victory of a man whom they detested, whom they dreaded to have as their archbishop. The chapter would have preferred to wait for the reply of the University of Paris, whose opinion had been requested. The answer of Paris was not in doubt; the Gallican party, the party of the University men and scholastic philosophers, could not be favorable to the Maid; a member of that party, the bishop of Coutances, had gone beyond all others in the harshness and strangeness of his answer. He wrote to the bishop of Beauvais that he considered her as a thrall of the devil, "because she did not possess the two qualities required by St. Gregory, virtue and humanity," and he added that her assertions were so heretical that even if she were to renounce them, she still ought to be kept under the strictest watch.

The all-important question was whether inner revelations must be silenced, must be disowned, when the Church so ordered. That question was debated in the open, and aloud. Was it not also fought over silently in the soul of the one who most staunchly affirmed and believed? Was not this battle of the faith waged within the very shrine of faith, within the loyal and simple heart of the Maid? I am inclined to believe it.

At times she declared she submitted to the pope, and requested she be sent to him. At times she drew a distinction, maintaining that in all matters of *faith* she was submissive to the pope, the prelates, the Church; but that concerning what she had *done*, she acknowledged no judge but God. At times, she gave up all distinctions, and, with no further explanation, she put her trust "in her King, the judge of heaven and earth."

Some may strive to throw a veil over these things, to conceal this human, fallible aspect in a figure they desire to be altogether holy; but her fluctuations are none the less apparent. It is unjustified to claim that the judges managed to mislead her in those questions. "She was very subtle," one of the witnesses shrewdly said, "with a woman's subtlety." I am tempted to ascribe to this inner combat the sickness which came upon her and brought her almost to the point of death. Her recovery did not take place until the time when her visions changed, when, as she herself told, Michael, the angel of battles, who was no longer sustaining her, yielded his place to Gabriel, the angel of grace and divine charity.

She fell sick during Holy Week. Her temptation may well have begun on Palm Sunday. A country girl, born close to the woods, she, who had constantly lived in the open, had to spend this lovely day, which the French call "Easter of the Flowers," in the depths of a dungeon. The great *aid* invoked by the Church [1] failed her; *the gate was not opened unto her.*

It opened on Tuesday, but only for the accused

[1] "Deus in *adjutorium* meum intende . . ." Palm Sunday, Prime.

to be brought before her judges in the great hall of the castle. They read to her the articles that had been drawn from her answers; and first of all the bishop represented to her "that all these doctors were clerics, scholars, versed in the law both human and divine; all of a kindly heart, and compassionate; that their desire was to proceed with gentleness, without seeking vengeance or *corporal punishment;* that they only wanted to enlighten her and set her on the right path of truth and salvation; that, as she was not properly instructed in such high matters, the bishop and the inquisitor offered that she should elect one or more of the assessors to act as her counsel." The accused, in presence of this assembly, among whom she could not descry a single friendly face, replied meekly: "In so far as you are admonishing me for my good and about our faith, I am grateful to you; as for the counsel you are offering me, I have no desire for any other counsel but that of Our Lord."

The first article dealt with the essential point, submission. She answered as before, "I believe indeed that our holy father, the bishops, and other clergy are appointed to maintain the Christian *faith* and to punish those who lapse from it. As for my *deeds*, I shall submit myself only to the Church in heaven, to God, to the Virgin, to the saints in paradise. I have not failed in my faith as a Christian, and I trust I shall never fail."

And later: "I would rather die than disown what I have done by Our Lord's Command."

It was characteristic of the time, of the doctors' narrowmindedness, of their blind attachment to the letter without any consideration for the spirit, that no point seemed more grievous to them than the sin of having assumed the garments of a man. They pointed out to her that according to the canons those who thus change the garb of their sex are an abomination in the sight of God. At first, she was reluctant to answer directly, and asked for a delay until the next day. As the judges were insisting upon her giving up her masculine attire, she replied that it did not depend upon her to say when she would be able to discard it.—"But if you were deprived of hearing mass?"—"Our Lord has it in His power for me to hear it without you."—"Would you not resume woman's clothes in order to receive your Saviour at Easter?"—"No, I cannot leave these clothes; to receive my Saviour, I make no difference between these garments and any others." Then she seemed shaken, and begged that she be at least allowed to hear Mass; and she added: "If only you would give me a gown such as the daughters of the well-to-do wear, a *very long gown*."

Here we understand what she blushed to explain. The poor girl was ashamed to say how she lived in her prison, in what perpetual danger. We must remember that three soldiers slept in her room, three of those brigands they called *houspilleurs* (roughnecks or goons). We must bear in mind that, shackled to a beam with a stout iron chain, she was almost at their mercy; the masculine garb that they wanted her to give up was her last protection. What can we say of the judge's obtuseness, or of his horrible conniving?

Under the eyes of these soldiers, exposed to their insults and their jeers, she was in addition spied upon from without; Winchester, the inquisitor, and Cauchon each had a key to the tower and observed her every hour; for that purpose, a hole had been bored in the wall; in that infernal dungeon, every stone had eyes.

Her sole comfort was that at first they had allowed a priest to communicate with her, a priest who pretended that he too was a prisoner and belonged to Charles VII's party. This Loyseleur ("bird catcher") as he was called was in fact a Norman, and on the English side. He had gained Joan's confidence, heard her in confession; and during that time, notaries, from a hiding place, were listening and writing down. . . . It is claimed that Loyseleur encouraged her to resist, so as to compass her destruction. When they discussed whether she should be put to torture (a useless step, since she was denying or concealing nothing), only two or three advised such an atrocity, and the confessor was one of them.

The deplorable state of the prisoner grew worse during Holy Week, as a result of her being denied religious comfort. On Thursday, she suffered from not being admitted to the Lord's Supper; on that day, when Christ bids all men to His table, when He invites the poor and the afflicted, she appeared to be *forgotten.*

On Good Friday, the day of universal silence, when in the solemn hush everyone hears only the beating of his own heart, it seems that the hearts of the judges did speak at last, that a sentiment of humanity and religion did stir their parched scholastic souls. One thing is certain: on Wednesday, thirty-five appeared at the hearing; on Saturday, only nine; the others no doubt gave as an excuse that they had to attend to their devotions.

She on the contrary had picked up courage; associating her sufferings with those of Christ, she recovered her assurance. She answered once more that "she would accept the rule of the Church militant, *provided she was not commanded anything impossible.*"—"Do you believe then that you are not subject to the Church on this earth, to our holy father the pope, to the cardinals, archbishops, bishops, prelates?"—"Certainly; *but first Our Lord must be served.*"—"Do your voices forbid you to submit to the Church militant?"—"They do not forbid it, if Our Lord be obeyed first of all."

V

The Temptation

This firmness did not waver on Saturday. But how did she fare on the next day, Sunday, that holiest of Sundays, Easter? What happened in her poor heart when the universal spirit of rejoicing broke forth tumultuously throughout the city, when the five hundred bells of Rouen rang out wild and joyous in the sky, when the Christian world was rising again with the Saviour, and she, she alone, remained a prey to death?

We may boast as proudly as we please, we philosophers and rationalists of the present age. But who among us, amid the agitations of the modern world, or in the voluntary servitude of research, in its harsh and lonely quest, who can hear without emotion the sound of these lovely Christian festivals, the voice of the bells touching our hearts like a mother's gentle reproof? . . . Who is able to watch without envy the faithful streaming out of the church, leaving the divine board rejuvenated, and as if created anew? . . . The mind remains firm, but the soul is sad unto death. . . . He who puts his faith in the future, but whose heart is obstinately attached to the past, drops his pen and closes his book; he cannot help confessing: "Ah! would I were with them, one of them, the simplest, the least among these children!" [1]

With what force would such a cruel isolation be felt, in that age! And most of all by a young soul that hitherto had lived by her faith alone! She who, for all her inner life of visions and revelations, had nonetheless obeyed unquestioningly the commands of the Church, she who up to that time had considered herself with naïve assurance as an obedient daughter of the Church, "a good and dutiful daughter," as she said—could she without terror become aware that the Church her mother stood against her?—Alone, at the time when all others were united in God, debarred alone from the joy and communion of all men, on the very day when the gates of Heaven opened for mankind—alone to be excluded!

And was this exclusion an injustice? A Christian soul is too humble to claim it deserves to receive its God. Who was she after all that she should contradict prelates and doctors? How did she dare to speak before so many men of wisdom and profound learning? When an ignorant girl resisted the scholars, when a mere peasant stood against those in high authority—

[1] This paragraph was omitted in the 1853 edition.

did not that argue overweening conceit and damnable pride? . . . Certainly, such fears must have come to her.

On the other hand, Joan's resistance was not hers alone, but that of the saints and the angels who had dictated her answers and sustained her hitherto. Why was it, alas, that they came more rarely now, in the hours of greatest need? Why did the comforting faces of the saints no longer appear except in a dubious light, which grew dimmer day by day? She had been promised deliverance: why did it tarry? Many a time, no doubt, the prisoner must have asked herself those questions; many a time, in a whisper, very gently, she must have reproved the saints and the angels. But when angels fail to keep their word, can they be angels of light? . . . Let us hope this horrible suspicion never entered her mind.

There was one means of escape. It consisted, without expressly repudiating her claims, in saying: "It seems to me." To the jurists, this appeared easy enough. But for her to speak such a word of doubt meant denying, abjuring her glorious dream of heavenly friendships, disowning her gentle sisters, the saints in Paradise. It were better to die. . . . And, in fact, rejected by the visible Church, forsaken by the invisible Church, by the world, by her own heart, the hapless girl was faltering. . . . And her body sickened with her soul.

That very day she happened to taste of a fish sent her by the charitable bishop of Beauvais; she may have thought she was poisoned. It would have been to the bishop's advantage; Joan's death would have ended this embarrassing trial; it would have extricated the judge. But the English felt differently. Lord Warwick said, in great alarm: "Not for anything in the world would the *king* have her die a natural death; the *king* has bought her, and the price was high! She must die a felon's death, she must be burnt at the stake. . . . See to it that she gets cured."

So they took great care of her; doctors visited her, she was cupped and bled; but she felt no better. She remained weak and at the point of death. Perhaps because they feared she would thus escape them and die without retracting anything, perhaps because they hoped that a weakened body would break down the resistance of her spirit, the judge made another attempt (April 8). They came to her in her cell, and pointed out that she stood in great danger, if she refused to take counsel from the Church and follow its advice. "It seems to me indeed," she said, "that my sickness is placing me in mortal peril. If it be so, may God deal with me as He pleases. I should like to make confession, to receive my Saviour, and to be buried in holy ground."—"If you want to receive the sacraments of the Church, you must do as all good Catholics do, and submit to the Church." She made no reply. Then, after the judge had repeated the same words, she said, "If my body dies while I am in prison, I hope you will have it laid in holy ground; if you do not, I leave it all to the Lord."

In the course of previous questionings, she had expressed one of her last desires. *Question:* "You say that you wear man's garments by God's command, and yet you want to have a woman's shift in case you die?"—*Answer:* "All I want is that it be long." This touching reply shows clearly enough that, in her desperate straits, her thoughts were less for her life than for her modesty.

For a long time the doctors went on preaching to the sick girl; and the one who had particularly assumed the task of exhorting her, a scholastic philosopher from Paris, Master Nicholas Midy, finally told her with some asperity: "If you will not obey the Church, you will be abandoned like a Saracen."—"I am a good Christian," she replied gently, "I have been duly baptized, and I shall die a good Christian."

These delays exasperated the English. Winchester had hoped, before the next campaign, to bring the trial to a close, to extort a confession from the prisoner, and thus to dishonor King Charles. After this moral blow he expected to recapture Louviers, to hold Normandy securely, to have full control of the Seine; then he would be able to go to Basel and wage the other war, the theological war, to take his seat in the council as the arbiter of Christendom, to make and unmake popes. With such tremendous prospects he had to waste precious moments waiting for what that woman would consent to say.

Cauchon, in his indiscretion, had chosen that time to offend the chapter of Rouen from which he de-

sired a decision against the Maid; he had allowed
people to call him "my lord archbishop" in anticipa-
tion. Winchester resolved, without waiting for those
evasive Normans, to resort directly to the supreme
theological authority, the University of Paris.

While waiting for the reply, new attempts
were made to break down the resistance of the accused; wile and terror were brought to bear. In a
second admonition (May 2) the preacher, Master
Châtillon, offered to have the validity of her apparitions submitted to people of her own party. She eluded
the trap. "I still refer my case," she said, "to my
judge, the King of heaven and earth." This time she
did not say, as she had before: "To God *and to the
pope.*" "Well then, the Church will abandon you,
and you will be in peril of fire, soul as well as body."
—"If you do as you say, evil shall come to your body
and to your soul."

They were not satisfied with vague threats. For
the third admonition, which took place in her cell on
May 11, they brought in the executioner, they affirmed that torture was in readiness. . . . But this
was of no avail. On the contrary, she recovered all
her courage and stood more firmly than ever. Up-
lifted in spirit after her temptation, she had, as it were,
ascended another step toward the fountain of grace.
"The angel Gabriel," she said, "has come to strengthen
me; it was he indeed, the saints have assured me that
it was. . . . God has ever been my lord in everything
I have done; never has the devil had any power over

me. . . . Even if you had my limbs drawn and quartered, and if you wrenched my soul from my body, I could not speak otherwise." The Spirit was so manifest in her that Châtillon himself, her latest opponent, was moved, and became her defender; he declared that in his opinion a trial so conducted was void. Cauchon, beside himself, ordered him to hold his peace.

Finally, the answer came from the University of Paris. It decided that on the matter of the twelve articles this girl was a thrall of the devil, without filial piety, athirst for Christian blood, etc. This was the opinion of the Theological School. The School of Law, more moderate, declared that she deserved punishment, but with two restrictions: (1) only if she remained obdurate, and (2) if she were of sound mind.

The University was writing at the same time to the pope, to the cardinals, to the king of England, praising the bishop of Beauvais, and declaring that "in its opinion, the whole procedure had been marked by great gravity, and conducted in a holy and equitable manner, wherewith every one should be well satisfied."

Armed with this answer, some were in favor of having the prisoner burned without any further delay; this might have satisfied the doctors, whose authority she had spurned, but not the English; what they wanted was a retractation that would brand King Charles with *infamy*. They tried a new admonition, a new preacher, Master Peter Morice, who met with no better success; in vain did he adduce the authority of the University of Paris, "the light of all science."—"Even though I saw the executioner and the fire," she said, "I could not say anything but what I have said."

Thus, the twenty-third of May was reached, the day after Whitsun. Winchester could no longer remain in Rouen; the matter must be brought to a close. They resolved to stage a great and terrible public scene, in order either to frighten the accused, or at any rate to impress and delude the people. They dispatched to her, the evening before, Loyseleur, Châtillon, and Morice, to promise her that if she were submissive, if she would quit wearing man's garments, she would be turned over to clerics and would no longer be in the hands of the English.

It was in the cemetery of St. Ouen, back of the handsome and austere monastic church (already built such as we see it today) [2] that the horrible farce was played. On a platform, Cardinal Winchester was seated with the two judges and thirty-three assessors, several having their scribes at their feet. On another platform, among the ushers and the torturers, was Joan, in man's garments; there were in addition notaries ready to take down her confession and a preacher to admonish her. At the foot, amid the crowd, a strange witness could be discerned: the executioner in his cart, ready to take her away as soon as judgment had been rendered.

The preacher of the day, a famous doctor, Wil-

[2] Since Michelet wrote this the main portal and the two spires of St. Ouen's were completed, with dubious success.

liam Erard, thought that on such a great occasion he
might give free rein to his eloquence, and his excess of
zeal spoilt everything. "O noble house of France," he
exclaimed, "hitherto the protector of the faith, how
could you be so deluded as to compromise yourself
with a heretic and schismatic. . . ." Up to that point,
the accused had listened with patience; but the
preacher, turning toward her, and lifting his finger,
said: "It is you, Joan, that I am addressing, and I tell
you that your king is a heretic and a schismatic." On
hearing these words, the noble girl, forgetting her
own danger, cried out: "By my faith, and saving your
reverence, I make bold to tell you and to swear, on
penalty of my life, that he is the noblest Christian
among all Christians; the one who loves best our
faith and the Church; he is not such as you call him."
—"Make her keep quiet," Cauchon cried.

So all these efforts, labors, expenses, had been
wasted. The accused held her ground. All they could
obtain from her at this time was that she was willing
to submit *to the pope.* Cauchon replied: "The pope is
too far." Then he started reading an act of condemnation which had been prepared in advance; among
other things, it said: "Worst of all, in the stubborn-
ness of your spirit, you have refused to submit *to the
Holy Father* and the council, etc." Meanwhile, Loyseleur and Erard were adjuring her to take pity on
herself; the bishop, his hope somewhat reviving, interrupted his reading. Then the English grew furious;
a secretary of Winchester told Cauchon that evidently

he favored that woman; the chaplain of the cardinal voiced the same thought. "You are lying!" the bishop cried. "And you," the other answered, "you are a traitor to the king." These grave personages seemed ready to come to blows right in their tribunal.

Erard was not discouraged, but kept pouring threats and entreaties. At times he would say, "Joan, we have such pity on you!" and then: "Abjure or you shall burn!" Everybody was taking a hand, even a kindly usher who, moved by compassion, was urging her to yield, assuring her that she would be taken out of the hands of the English and delivered to the Church. "Well then, I shall sign," she said. Then Cauchon, turning to the cardinal, asked him respectfully what was to be done. "Admit her to penitence," the prince of the Church replied.

Winchester's secretary pulled out of his sleeve a very short recantation in six lines (the one which was published later filled six pages). He placed a pen in her hand, but she did not know how to sign; she smiled and traced a circle; the secretary took hold of her hand and made her draw a cross.

The sentence "of grace" was in fact of the utmost rigor: "Joan, we condemn you, in our grace and moderation, to spend the rest of your days in prison, on the bread of sorrow and the water of affliction, there to mourn for your sins."

She was admitted by the ecclesiastical judge to do penance: it could not be anywhere but in a Church prison. Hard as the Church dungeon (*in pace*) might be, this meant at least that she would be released from the custody of the English, that she would be protected from their insults, that her virtue would be safe. We may imagine her surprise and her despair when the bishop coldly said, "Take her back whence you brought her."

Nothing was achieved: thus deceived, she could not fail to retract her retractation. But even if she had allowed it to stand, the English in their rage would not have permitted it. They came to St. Ouen's in the hope that at last the witch would be burnt; they had waited, panting; and now they were to be put off with a scrap of parchment, a signature, a mockery. At the very moment when the bishop paused in the reading of the condemnation, stones were hurled upon both platforms, with no respect for the cardinal. The doctors were in danger of their lives when they stepped down upon the square; everywhere naked swords were at their throats. The most moderate among the English confined themselves to insulting words: "Priests, you are not earning the King's money." The doctors, slinking away in haste, said trembling, "Do not be uneasy: we shall get her yet."

And it was not only the common soldiery, the English *mob*, that evinced that thirst for blood. Substantial people, men of high station, the lords, were as savage as the rabble. The king's man, his governor, Lord Warwick, was saying like the soldiers, "Ill fares the king in all this: the woman is not to be burnt."

Warwick was exactly the man of good breeding

according to English standards, the accomplished pattern of an Englishman, the perfect *gentleman*. Brave and devout like his master Henry V, a zealous champion of the *established* Church, he had made a pilgrimage to the Holy Land and many another chivalric journey, never missing the chance of a tournament on his way. He himself gave one of the most dazzling and most famous of tourneys before the gates of Calais, challenging the whole chivalry of France. This festival left a long memory; the bravery, the magnificence displayed by this Warwick helped considerably in paving the way for the more famous Warwick, *the Kingmaker*.

In spite of his chivalrousness, Warwick was nonetheless relentlessly bent on compassing the death of a woman, of a war prisoner. The English, and even he who was the best among them, and the most highly esteemed, had no qualms about killing, through the sentence of a priest and at the stake, the Maid who had humbled them with the sword.

This people of England, with its greatness and its many good and solid virtues, suffers from a vice which spoils those very virtues. This vice, boundless and profound, is pride: a cruel disease, which is nonetheless their principle of life, the key to their antinomies, the secret of their actions. With them, virtues and vices are invariably founded upon pride, and their ludicrous aspects have the same origin. Their pride is prodigiously sensitive and painful; it causes them to suffer intensely, and they take further pride in concealing their suffering. However, the suffering does break out; the English language has two expressive words of its own, which the French have borrowed, *disappointment* and *mortification*.

This ego worship, this inner cult of the creature for its own self, such is the sin which caused the downfall of Satan, the supreme defiance of God. With so many virtues on the human plane, with their high seriousness, with their dignified bearing, with their biblical turn of mind, no people stands farther away from grace than the English. From Shakespeare to Milton, from Milton to Byron, their literature, in its somber beauty, is skeptical, Judaic, satanic. "With regard to the law," a jurist rightly said, "the English are Jews, the French are Christians." What he said of the law, a theologian could have said of the faith. The American Indians, who often reveal so much penetration and originality, expressed this distinction in their own way: "Christ," said one of them, "was a Frenchman whom the English crucified in London; Pontius Pilate was an official in the service of Great Britain."

Never were the Jews filled with such hatred against Jesus as the English against the Maid. She had, we must admit, wounded them at their most sensitive point, in the naïve and profound esteem they have of themselves. At Orleans their invincible men-at-arms and their famous archers with Talbot at their head had turned tail; at Jargeau, in a fortified town behind stout walls they had allowed themselves to be caught;

at Patay, they had fled as fast as their legs could carry them, fled before a girl. These memories were hateful to the English, who in their taciturn pride kept chewing the bitter cud. . . . A girl had filled them with fear; it was not certain that even now, chained though she was, they were not still afraid of her. . . . Not of her, of course, but of the devil whose agent she was; at least that was what they were trying to believe and to make others believe.

There was, however, one objection to their claim: she was reputed to be a virgin, and it was a notorious, a well-established fact that the devil could not enter into a pact with a virgin. The wisest head among the English, the regent, Bedford, resolved to clear up this point; the duchess his wife sent matrons, who reported that in fact Joan was a maid. This favorable declaration turned against her, for it gave rise to another superstitious fancy. They concluded that her virginity was the key to her strength and power; if she were robbed of it, she would be disarmed, the spell would be broken, she would sink to the common level of women.

The poor girl, in such a danger, had so far had no protection but her man's attire. But, strangely enough, no one was willing to understand why she chose to wear it. Friends and foes found it a cause of scandal. Right at the beginning, she had been obliged to explain the case to the women of Poitiers. After she was captured, and placed under the guard of the Luxemburg ladies, these worthy dames entreated her to dress as a well-behaved girl should. The English women in particular, always so punctilious when chastity and modesty are concerned, must have considered such a change of garments as something monstrous and intolerably indecent. The duchess of Bedford sent her a woman's gown—but with whom? with a man, a tailor. That man, free and familiar, ventured to slip the gown on her, and as she repulsed him, he made bold to lay his hand on hers, a tailor's hand on the hand that had carried the flag of France. She slapped his face.

If women failed to understand this feminine problem, what could be expected of the priests? They quoted a text from a fourth-century council, declaring anathema such changes of attire. They failed to realize that this prohibition applied with particular force in a period which was barely emerging from pagan impurity. The doctors who belonged to the party of Charles VII, the apologists of the Maid, found it difficult to justify her on this point; one of them asserts, without a shred of evidence, that as soon as she dismounted she assumed again a woman's garb. He confessed that Esther and Judith made use of more natural, more feminine means to overcome the enemies of the Lord's own people. These theologians, concerned exclusively with the soul, seem to have paid scant attention to the body; if only you follow the letter, the written law, the soul will be saved; let the flesh fare as it may. . . . A poor simple girl must be forgiven if she failed to understand these subtle distinctions.

It is our harsh fate on earth that body and soul should be so closely bound together; that the soul should have to drag the body along, should be exposed to its vicissitudes, should even respond to them. This primal curse has always weighed heavily upon us; but how much more heavily under a religious law which compels us to endure this outrageous condition; which will not permit our honor, when it is imperiled, to save itself by casting aside the body, and seeking refuge in the world of the spirit!

VI

Joan's Death

On Friday and Saturday the wretched prisoner, deprived of her male garments, had much to fear. Brutal nature, furious hatred, vengeance, everything would urge the cowards to degrade her before she perished, to sully the victim they were going to burn. . . . They might be tempted to cover their infamy with a *raison d'état*, according to the ideas of the time; by ravishing her virginity, they would destroy the occult power of which they were so horribly afraid; it might restore their courage to realize that after all she was but a woman. According to her confessor, to whom she had revealed the fact, an Englishman, not a common soldier, but a gentleman, a lord, had patriotically assumed the task; he had bravely attempted to rape a girl in chains; and when he did not succeed, he had showered her with blows.

When Sunday morning came, Trinity Sunday, and she had to rise, as she reported to a witness,[1] she

[1] The usher Massieu, who followed her right to the stake.

told her English guards, "Take off my shackles, so that I may get up." One of them took off the woman's garments she wore, emptied a bag containing man's clothing, and said to her, "Arise."—"Gentlemen," she said, "you know I am forbidden to wear this; excuse me, but I will not put it on." The discussion went on until noon; finally, a bodily necessity compelled her to go out, and to take the clothes given her. When she came back, they would not give her any other, in spite of all her entreaties.

It was not actually to the advantage of the English that she should resume the wearing of man's clothing, thus canceling the recantation that had been so hard to obtain. But at that moment their rage knew no bounds. Saintrailles had boldly attempted a raid on Rouen. It would have been a splendid stroke to snatch the judges right from their tribunal, to take Winchester and Bedford to Poitiers; Bedford had another narrow escape on his way back from Rouen to Paris. The English felt insecure so long as the accursed woman was alive; undoubtedly, she kept weaving her evil spells in her prison. She must perish.

The assessors, summoned at once to the castle to certify that she had changed to man's clothes again, found in the courtyard some hundred Englishmen who barred their way; they thought that these doctors, if allowed to enter, would spoil the game; they raised their battle-axes and their swords against them and chased them away, calling them *Armagnac traitors*. Cauchon managed with great difficulty to be

admitted; he affected gaiety in order to please Warwick, and said with a laugh, "She is caught."

On Monday he returned with the inquisitor and
eight assessors to question the Maid and ask her why
she had resumed those garments. She offered no excuse, but, bravely facing her peril, she said that this
garb was more suitable, so long as she had men as her
keepers, and that besides the judges had failed to keep
their word to her. Her saints had told her that "it was
a great pity she had abjured in order to save her life."
However, she was not refusing to wear woman's
clothes. "Give me a safe and mild prison," she said,
"and I shall be good, and obey the Church in everything."

The bishop, as he left, met Warwick, and to
show his loyalty to the English cause he said in
English, "Farewell, farewell." This cheerful good-bye
meant something like "it is all over."

On Tuesday the judges summoned to the archbishop's palace a hotchpotch assembly, some assessors
who had been present only at the first meetings, some
who had never attended at all; men of all sorts, clerics,
jurists, and even three medical men. The judges reported to the assembly what had taken place and
requested its opinion. The opinion, very different
from what had been expected, was that the prisoner
should be summoned once more, and that her act of
abjuration should be read over to her. It is doubtful
whether the judges had any authority to do this. In
reality, in the tumult of the raging soldiery and the

clanking of swords there were no judges any more, and no judicial process was possible. The mob was howling for blood; perhaps the judges would have been the first victims. They drew up in haste a summons to be delivered on the morrow at eight o'clock; she was not to appear again, save to be burnt.

In the morning, Cauchon sent her a confessor, Brother Martin l'Advenu, "to apprise her of her coming death and induce her to penitence. . . ." When he told the poor woman what manner of death was awaiting her, she cried out most piteously, flung her arms about and tore her hair, "Alas! Am I to be treated with such horrible cruelty, that my body, wholly pure and never sullied, should be consumed today and turned into ashes! Ah! I should prefer to be beheaded seven times over than to be burnt in this wise! . . . Oh! I appeal to God, the great judge, to right the wrongs and grievances done to me!"

After this outburst of grief, she recovered herself, made confession, and asked to receive communion. The friar was in a predicament; but the bishop, whom he consulted, answered that she might be given communion, "and anything she might desire." Thus, at the very moment he had pronounced her a heretic and a backslider, and as such cut off from the Church, he was granting her that which the Church gives to the faithful. Perhaps a last sentiment of humanity rose in the heart of the wicked judge; he may have thought he had done enough in having the poor creature burnt, without casting her into despair and damnation. Perhaps the bad priest, with the indifferent levity of a skeptic, was allowing her the sacraments as something of little consequence, which might simply soothe the victim, and induce her to hold her peace. At first they attempted to go through with the ceremony surreptitiously, the host was brought without stole and without tapers. But the monk complained, and the churchmen of Rouen, duly informed, took advantage of this to express their opinion of Cauchon's judgment; they sent the body of Christ by the light of many torches, escorted by numerous priests who chanted litanies and told the people kneeling along the streets, "Pray for her."

After receiving communion with abundant tears, she caught sight of the bishop and said to him, "Bishop, my death is your doing. . . ." And again, "If you had placed me in a Church prison and in the keeping of ecclesiastics, this would not have happened. . . . That is why I appeal against you before God!"

Then, noticing among those in attendance Peter Morice, one of those who had preached to her, she said to him, "Ah! Master Peter, where shall I be tonight?"—"Do you not have a firm hope in the Lord?"—"Oh! yes, with God's help, I shall be in Paradise."

It was nine. They had clothed her in woman's garb and put her on a cart. By her side stood her confessor, Brother Martin l'Advenu; Massieu, the usher, was on her other side. The Augustinian monk,

Brother Isambart, who had already shown such charity and such courage, would not relinquish her. It was asserted that the wretched Loyseleur also climbed onto the cart, to beg her forgiveness; the English would have killed him but for the Earl of Warwick's intervention.

Up to that moment the Maid had never despaired, except perhaps in her hour of temptation during Holy Week. While saying as she sometimes did, "These English people will put me to death," at bottom she did not believe it. She did not imagine that she would be abandoned. She had faith in her king, in the good people of France. She had said it expressly, "There will be in the prison, or at the time of the judgment, a great commotion whereby I shall be freed . . . delivered through a great victory! . . ." But even if king and people failed her, she had another support, infinitely more powerful and more assured, that of her friends from on high, her kind and beloved saints. . . . When she was besieging St. Peter, and her soldiers abandoned her at the moment of the assault, the saints sent an invisible army to her aid. How could they now forsake their obedient daughter, they who so often had promised her rescue and deliverance!

What must have been her thoughts then, when she saw that of a certainty she was going to die, when she was carried in the cart through a quivering multitude, under the guard of eight hundred Englishmen armed with spears and swords? She wept and mourned; yet she accused neither her king nor her saints. . . . Only these words escaped her lips: "O Rouen, Rouen! Is it here that I must die?"

The end of this sorrowful journey was the Old Market Place, the fish market. Three platforms had been erected. On the first was the episcopal and royal chair, the throne of the English cardinal, and beside it the seats of his prelates. On the second were to figure the characters in the somber drama, the preacher, the judge, the bailiff, and the condemned. Apart from these, there rose a huge mass of plaster heaped high with wood; they had not been niggardly with the pyre: its height filled the spectators with awe. This was not done merely to give the execution a more solemn character: there was another motive. The pyre had been made so high, so that the executioner could only reach its base; he would not be able to shorten the torture, and mercifully to dispatch the victim, as he usually did, and so to spare her the flames. In this case, they wanted to make sure that justice would not be cheated, that the fire would not simply devour a corpse; they wanted her to be literally burnt alive; they wanted her, hoisted atop this mountain of fuel, above the encircling spears and swords, to be in plain sight for everyone in the market place. The slow, protracted burning under the eyes of the watchful crowd would probably expose at last some flaw, would wrench from her some cries that might be given out as a recantation, at the very least some confused, barely articulate words that could be so twisted; perhaps some craven prayer, some humiliating appeal to mercy, such as one would expect from a woman demented with terror.

A chronicler, a friend of the English, here lays a heavy charge against them. If we are to believe him, they wanted her dress to be consumed first, revealing her nakedness, "so as to remove all doubts from the minds of the people"; the fire being brushed aside for a moment, everyone could draw nigh and stare at her, "and all the secrets which may or should be in a woman's body"; after this immoral and ferocious exhibition, the executioner was to make the flames blaze anew on her poor carcass."

The horrible ceremony began with a sermon. Master Nicholas Midy, one of the lights of the University of Paris, preached on the edifying text: "When one limb of the Church is sick, the whole Church is sick." The poor Church could be healed only by cutting off the limb. He concluded with the formula: "Joan, go *you* in peace, the Church can no longer defend *thee*."

Then the ecclesiastical judge, the bishop of Beauvais, exhorted her with benignity to care for her soul and to remember all her transgressions, so as to rouse herself to contrition. The assessors had ruled that according to the law her abjuration should be read over to her; the bishop omitted this. He was afraid she would give him the lie, raise a protest. But the poor girl had little thought of thus haggling for her life; her mind was fixed on very different things. Even be-

fore she had been exhorted to contrition, she had fallen
on her knees, invoking God, the Virgin, St. Michael
and St. Catherine, forgiving everyone and asking
forgiveness; begging of the crowd that they pray for
her. Above all, she entreated every one of the priests
present to say a mass for her soul. All this in such a
devout, humble and touching fashion that all were
moved and could not repress their feelings; the bishop
of Beauvais began weeping, the bishop of Boulogne
was sobbing, and now even the English were in tears,
Winchester like the rest.

Might it be that in that moment of universal
tenderness, of tears, of contagious weakness, the hapless girl, softened, relapsing into mere womanhood,
did confess that now she could see clearly she had
been wrong, that they had deceived her who had
promised deliverance? On this point, we cannot accept
with implicit faith the biased testimony of the English.
But it would betray scant knowledge of human nature
to doubt that, frustrated as she was in her hope, her
faith may have wavered. Did she actually utter the
words? The thing is not certain; but I dare to affirm
that the thought was there.

Meanwhile, the judges, dismayed for a moment,
had rallied and were their stern selves again; the
bishop of Beauvais, wiping his eyes, began reading the
sentence. He rehearsed for the culprit all her crimes
—schism, idolatry, invoking demons; how, after being
admitted to penitence, she was "seduced by the Prince
of lies and had relapsed, O grief! *like the dog return-*

ing to his vomit! . . . Therefore, we pronounce you
a rotten limb, and as such cut off from the Church;
we deliver you over to the secular power, *begging it
however to be mild in dealing with you, and to spare
you death and bodily mutilation.*"

Thus rejected by the Church, she committed herself in full confidence to God. She asked for a cross.
An Englishman made a wooden one out of a stick,
and handed it to her; she received it devoutly, crude
as it was, and placed it under her garments, next to
her skin. . . . But she desired a regular Church crucifix to keep before her eyes until the moment of
death. The kindly usher, Massieu, and Brother Isambart pleaded so earnestly that a cross was brought to
her from the parish church of St. Saviour. As she was
clasping the cross, and as Isambart was comforting
her, the English began to grow weary of the delay; it
must have been past noon; the soldiers were grum-
bling; the captains growled, "What's all this, you
priests? Do you mean us to stay here till dinner
time? . . ." Then, losing patience, and without waiting for the order of the bailiff, who alone had the
authority to send her to death, they had two sergeants
climb the platform and snatch her from the hands of
the priests. At the foot of the tribunal, she was seized
by men-at-arms, who dragged her to the executioner,
and told him, "Do your office. . . ." The fury of the
soldiers roused a feeling of horror; many in the crowd,
and even some of the judges, ran away, unable to bear
the sight any more.

When she was brought down from the platform to the market place, roughly handled by the English soldiers, nature broke down, and the flesh in her was perturbed; she cried anew, "O Rouen, so thou art to be my last abode! . . ." She said no more, and *did not sin with her lips*, in this hour of terror and agony.

She accused neither her king, nor her saints. But when she had reached the top of the pyre, and saw the vast city, the motionless and silent crowd, she could not help saying, "Ah! Rouen, Rouen, I sadly fear thou wilt suffer because of my death!" She who had saved the people, and whom the people were forsaking, in the admirable sweetness of her soul, had only words of compassion for the people, as she was about to die.

She was tied under the placard of infamy; a miter placed on her head with the words: "Heretic, back-slider, apostate, idolater. . . ." The executioner lit the fire. She saw it from her high station and uttered a cry. Then, as the friar who was exhorting her was paying no heed to the flames, she, forgetting herself, was afraid for him and bade him descend.

The proof that up to that moment she had made no formal recantation is that the wretched Cauchon felt obliged (impelled no doubt by the supreme satanic will which presided over the whole) to come to the foot of the pyre, forced to confront his victim once more, in a last effort to wrest from her some damning admission. He drew but these words, fit to rack his soul—words that she had told him before, and which she repeated with gentleness, "Bishop, my death is your doing. . . . If you had placed me in

a prison of the Church, this would not have come to
pass." They may have hoped that, believing herself
abandoned by her king, she would accuse him at last,
and speak against him. But even then, she was defend-
ing him still: "Whether I have done well or ill, my
king is not at fault; it was not he who counseled me."

Meanwhile the flames were rising. At the moment they reached her she shivered and in her agony
cried for holy *water; water*, it was probably a cry
wrenched by terror. But soon conquering herself, she
had only the names of God, her angels and her saints
on her lips, "Yes, my voices came from God, my
voices did not deceive me! . . ." All doubt vanished
in the flames; this leads us to believe that she had accepted death as the promised *deliverance*, that she no
longer understood *salvation* in the Judaic, literal,
material sense, as she had done hitherto, that she saw
the light at last, and that, as she emerged from the dark
shadows, her gifts of illumination and sanctity were
fully purified and attained their supreme perfection.

These great words of hers are vouched for by
the one who was the official and sworn witness of her
death—the Dominican who went with her up the pile,
whom she requested to go down, and who, from below, spoke to her, listened to her, held the cross before
her eyes.

We have another testimony on her holy death, a
witness of the most unimpeachable authority. This
man, whose name history must preserve and honor,
was the Augustinian monk we have mentioned before, Brother Isambart de la Pierre; during the trial,

he came near being put to death because he had advised the Maid; yet, although so clearly exposed to the hatred of the English, he insisted on climbing into the cart with her; he had the parish crucifix brought to her; he comforted her in the midst of the raging multitude, both on the platform and at the stake.

Twenty years later, the two religious, plain monks, who had espoused poverty, without anything to gain or to fear in this world, testified to the scene we have just described, "We could hear her," they said, "in the fire, invoking her saints, her archangel; she kept repeating the name of our Saviour. . . . Finally, her head dropped, and she uttered a great cry: 'Jesus!' "

"Ten thousand men were weeping. . . ." Only a few Englishmen laughed, or were trying to laugh. One of them, among the most furious, had sworn he would lay a faggot on the pyre; she was expiring at the time he put it, and he swooned; his comrades took him to a tavern, to make him drink and revive his spirits; but he could not recover. "I saw," he said, beside himself, "I saw with her last breath a dove fly out of her mouth." Others had read in the flames the name she was repeating: "Jesus!" The executioner that evening sought Brother Isambart; he was terror-stricken; he made confession, but he could not believe that God would ever forgive him. A secretary of the king of England, as he returned, said aloud, "We are lost, we have burnt a saint."　　　✠ ✠ ✠

I have followed the text of the edition in a separate volume (1853); but I have restored the key paragraph [1] so unfortunately deleted by Michelet. I have adopted the division into six chapters, as a definite improvement on the earlier one.

Numerous footnotes appear in both editions. Some of them introduce interesting if minor points, but most of them are references to sources. I have left them out without hesitation. Michelet's book has achieved a permanent place in historical literature, both as a beautiful story beautifully told, and as a masterly interpretation of a simple yet mysterious figure. It is substantially accurate, but as a work of erudition it has no standing. The readers interested in research are referred to Gustave Rudler's critical edition and to his *Michelet Historien de Jeanne d'Arc*.[2] I have added a few notes, when they seemed to me indispensable to the understanding of the text.

The narrative begins and ends somewhat abruptly, since it was extracted from a larger work. From the artistic point of view, this is no blemish. In the 1853 edition, Michelet added an Introduction and a Conclusion. These, however, are reflections of a moral nature, almost lay sermons, and do not provide the required historical background. For the English or American reader, they contribute nothing essential to the intelligence and enjoyment of the narrative.

[1] "The Temptation," pp. 94–95 of the present text.
[2] *Vide supra*, Introduction, pp. vii–viii.

THE HISTORICAL BACKGROUND

French children are painfully familiar with the principal events of the Hundred Years' War; or at any rate, they were in my days. Foreign readers may easily be excused if their recollections of that protracted and chaotic conflict are a trifle blurred. Crécy, Calais, Poitiers, Agincourt, Orleans are familiar names; but not a few well-educated people could not tell off-hand who the Armagnacs were or what the Cabochiens stood for. I offer a brief and inevitably rough sketch of the whole period. The genealogical table herein will make the rival claims of Valois and Plantagenets a little less bewildering.

The conquest of England by the French Normans (no longer Norsemen) created a paradoxical situation. The duke of Normandy, with a royal title like his suzerain, with a more compact territory and a more firmly knit authority, chafed at his position of vassalage. The conflict began with William the Conqueror himself. A great stroke of luck upset the balance in favor of England: Eleanor of Aquitania, repudiated by Louis VII of France, married in 1152 Henry Plantagenet, count of Anjou and duke of Normandy, who two years later became king of England as Henry II. The Angevin empire, in addition to England and its vast French domains, claimed suzerainty over Brittany, Wales, Scotland, and part of Ireland.

France took the upper hand again when sagacious Philip Augustus was matched against Richard the Lion-Hearted and the craven John Lackland. St. Louis assuaged the bitter rivalry in saintly and unrealistic fashion; although victorious, he restored to the English king some of his continental possessions (Paris, 1259). This long spasmodic struggle has been called the First Hundred Years' War.[3] The English dynasty, long rooted in France, still French-speaking, with French as the language of the courts and of the nobility, could not easily forget or forego its splendid French heritage.

Between 1314 and 1328, three brothers, the last of the direct Capetian line, died without male issue;[4] the situation had never occurred in the 341 years of Capetian rule. Edward III of England, through his mother Isabella, was actually the next of kin: the nephew of the last three kings, the grandson of Philip the Fair. But an assembly of peers and barons declared that, "according to custom, no woman, nor therefore her son, could succeed to the monarchy of France." This was by no means a general rule under feudalism. Eleanor of Aquitania had inherited her duchy without demur, and there had been queens in their own rights on many European thrones. This questionable decision was later called the Salic law; but the French had forgotten for some eight hundred years that they had ever been Salian Franks.

A distant cousin of the late king, Philip of Va-

---

[3] The second raged, fitfully, from 1337 to 1453; the third, almost as continuous, from 1688 to 1815.

[4] John I died at birth (1316).

lois, was called to the throne as Philip VI. Edward III did not at once press his claims. But Valois and Plantagenets remained rivals. Their dynastic conflict was embittered by economic considerations. England could not live in splendid isolation; she needed both Flanders and Guienne as markets. The wool she sold in Bruges paid for the wine she bought in Bordeaux.

After a few years of sparring in Flanders and in Brittany, the rivals came into open warfare. Philip VI, with his numerous, brilliant, and undisciplined cavalry, suffered a crushing defeat at Crécy (1346). In 1347 Edward III captured Calais, which was to remain in English hands until 1558. John the Good, an even worse ruler, was made prisoner at Poitiers (1356) by the son of Edward III, the Black Prince.

It looked as though military disaster might lead to civil reforms: the States General (1355–56) and Etienne Marcel, Provost of the Paris merchants, gave adumbrations of the French Magna Carta. The peasants, or *Jacques*, were rising in wild rebellion. But the Estates fumbled, Etienne Marcel perished, and the dauphin, determined under his unpromising appearance, managed to extricate himself. The treaty of Brétigny (1360) ceded more French provinces to Edward III.

The dauphin, regent during his father's captivity, became king as Charles V in 1364. He deserved to be called the Wise. Frail, studious, cautious, a careful administrator and a shrewd diplomat, ably seconded in the field by his constable Bertrand du Guesclin, he

recovered province after province without any spec-
tacular triumph. Edward III in his dotage and Richard Yea-and-Nay were no match for him. When he
died in 1380, the English held only five "pockets,"
Bayonne, Bordeaux, Brest, Cherbourg and Calais.

The endemic war was quiescent for thirty-five
years. Richard II and Henry IV were incapable of a
spirited policy. But in France, after a fair start,
Charles VI went mad. His uncles were squandering
the substance of the realm; Orleans and Burgundy,
in particular, were fighting bitterly for the spoils. The
duke of Orleans was killed in 1407 by order of John
the Fearless, duke of Burgundy; but his son, who had
married the daughter of the count of Armagnac, kept
up the feud. In 1413, Burgundy gained the upper
hand in Paris. His faction was supported by the rough
followers of the skinner, or knacker, Simon Caboche.
Strangely enough, this demagogic element and the
great University of Paris united in passing an intelligent charter, the great "Cabochien" Ordinance. But
Burgundy was driven out of Paris, the Orleans-
Armagnac faction seized control, and a White Terror
reigned in the city from December, 1413, until July,
1414.

These tragic divisions gave Henry V of England
his chance. A young, ambitious, and able prince, he
was eager to give prestige to his usurping house, Lancaster. He landed at Harfleur in 1415. Once more the
unruly mob of French knights-at-arms was shattered
by the small, well-armed, well-disciplined troops of

England—Henry V's "happy few"—at Agincourt.

The victory was brilliant, but in no sense decisive: all that Henry V could achieve, with his starved and tattered host, was to reach Calais and safety. The turn of the tide came later. John the Fearless had reentered Paris, and wrought massive retaliation on the Armagnacs and their partisans. He wanted, however, to seek reconciliation with his enemies; but the appointed meeting at Montereau Bridge was a trap, and he was felled with an ax by a hired agent of the Armagnacs (1419). Philip the Good, his son, and the whole Burgundian party went over bodily to the English side. The queen herself, Isabella of Bavaria, rallied to Henry V, who had married the king's daughter Catherine. She disowned and disinherited her own son the dauphin: by the treaty of Troyes (1420), Henry V became the heir apparent. When both Charles VI and Henry V died in 1422, the son of Henry and Catherine, the baby Henry VI, was proclaimed king of France and England. The duke of Burgundy, at that time the richest prince in Christendom, the *Parlement* or High Court of Paris, the University, "light of the Christian world," acknowledged the Lancastrian king.

It was France's darkest hour. The dauphin, listless except in pleasure seeking, held precariously but a few provinces in central France: he was derisively called "the king of Bourges." But the English, under a child, and far from united at home, were insecure in their triumph. Bedford, regent in France, won victories at Cravant (1423) and Verneuil (1424), but he did not follow them up. For nearly four years he remained inactive. At last, in 1428, his troops laid siege to Orleans, the key city, whose fall would have destroyed Charles VII's last chance. It was the Verdun, the Stalingrad of the Valois monarchy. Then Joan of Arc arose.

Accustomed as we are to national conflicts, we must bear in mind that the contest in those days was not sharply defined on such lines. Valois, Plantagenet or Lancaster, Navarre (Charles the Bad hovered ominously for a while), Burgundy, were all French-speaking princes, and all descendants of the Capetians. The capital, with its legal and theological authorities, had accepted Henry VI. The soldiery, whether English, Armagnac, or Burgundian, displayed the same impartial ferocity. Had Joan been born in a different village, she would have been a loyal Burgundian. When the king of her choice ultimately won the war, he became *France,* and this made her a national, not a factional, heroine. It might easily have been otherwise. That St. Margaret and St. Catherine, St. Michael and St. Gabriel came down from heaven in support of the shadowy Salic law strains credibility. But there is no major and no minor miracle: when reason is hushed, faith has a free field.

THE AFTERMATH

Michelet describes with contagious zest the enthusiasm, the crusading spirit that rallied the French to the cause of Charles VII. He tells us also, but in subdued tones, that this enthusiasm was short-lived. The miraculous career of the Maid lasted but a few weeks. She failed before Paris. In the winter of 1429–30, she was no longer a messenger from on high, but a captain among others, engaged in minor operations, and not brilliantly successful. When she was captured and sold to the English, the king who was the center of her faith did nothing to save her.

It is a sobering, indeed a distressing thought that this splendid epic actually was of little consequence; it was as barren as Roncesvalles and Roland's heroic death. France had succumbed because of Burgundy's defection. She recovered only because, six long years after the Maid's meteoric campaign, the man who had sold her, Philip the Good of Burgundy, chose to make his peace with France (Arras, 1435). He imposed his own terms; he was acknowledged as a sovereign prince for his lifetime. So powerful was he that his son Charles the Bold nearly got the better of crafty Louis XI. Only as a result of this reconciliation, Paris was recovered in 1436. But in spite of the deplorable conditions that weakened England in her turn, the French did not spontaneously rise to liberate themselves in the spirit of Joan of Arc. Normandy was not won until 1450 (Formigny), and Guienne not until 1453 (Castillon). Even then, Bordeaux, connected with England for nearly three hundred years, did not submit without a long siege and remained sullen for a whole generation.

So the marvelous story of Joan of Arc appears to the realistic historian as a luminous episode in a dark welter of incompetence, folly, assassination, and treachery, followed at last by a slow, unsensational recovery: Charles VII was rightly called the Well-Served. Miracles happen, but they do not explain.

Joan was—and this is perhaps the greatest of her miracles—prophetic in her political views. She stood for "France" against "England," at a time when there was no such clear-cut division. She stood for a king by right divine, and therefore absolute, in an age which was still feudal. In the fifteenth century, she was a dynastic nationalist, even as Cavour and Bismarck were.

It is by no means certain that her double ideal was the only one conceivable at the time, or indeed the most desirable. Paradox-mongers—one of my teachers, Camille Guy, was among them—might say that but for her intervention England and France would have remained united under a dynasty of French origin: thus realizing as early as 1422 the dream of Saint-Simon in 1814 and the desperate proposal of Winston Churchill in 1940. To equate king and country led to the worst excesses of Louis XIV: the French Revolution was directed against the spirit of Joan of Arc. To believe that the king's anointing conferred upon him a sacred character and supernatural powers is to raise Friedrich Sieburg's question: "Is God a Frenchman?" Perhaps Etienne Marcel and even the Cabochiens had a saner view of France's future. Hero worship is not wisdom; biography is not history—but it is far more entrancing.

Joan of Arc was rehabilitated by papal decree, in 1456, after a long inquiry promoted by the king. On January 27, 1894, the slow process of canonization was formally begun. On January 6, 1904, Pope Pius X declared Joan entitled to the designation *Venerable*. On December 13, 1908, the decree of *beatification* was published; in 1920, the prophecy of the English king's secretary, so heartily endorsed by Michelet, was fulfilled at last, and Pope Benedict XV declared Joan of Arc a saint.